The COUNTRY MUSIC
Book of Lists

The COUNTRY MUSIC Book of Lists

Fred Dellar and Richard Wootton

Times
BOOKS

On the cover

Front: Willie Nelson (Photo: Terry Lott)
Back: Merle Haggard

Published by TIMES BOOKS,
The New York Times Book Co, Inc.
130 Fifth Avenue, New York, N.Y. 10011

Published simultaneously in Canada by
Fitzhenry & Whiteside, Ltd., Toronto

Library of Congress Cataloging in Publication Data

Dellar, Fred.
  The country music book of lists.

  1. Country music—Miscellanea.   I. Wootton, Richard.
II. Title.
ML3524.D45   1984   784.5′2   84-40110
ISBN 0-8129-6339-3

Printed in Great Britain

84 85 86 87 88 5 4 3 2 1

Contents

Everything in *The Country Music Book of Lists* is a list – and that starts here, with the songs that we've used for our list headings. To find out the names of the artists who recorded them, turn to the very last list in the book on page 171.

The authors, Richard Wootton *2nd from left* and Fred Dellar *3rd from left*, with the
Oak Ridge Boys

ALL THESE THINGS

Introduction

Why would Janie Fricke like to take President Reagan to a desert island? When was Gene Autry nearly killed by a Muranian death-ray? What are Boxcar Willie's favorite train songs? Who recorded such dotty ditties as "My Head Hurts, My Feet Stink And I Don't Love Jesus" and "My Uncle Used to Love Me but She Died"? Which Country star is named after a hamburger chain? These are just a few of the thousands of questions we've sought to answer in *The Country Music Book of Lists*.

In our search we went to the stars themselves and requested people like The Oak Ridge Boys, George Hamilton IV, The Gatlin Brothers, George Jones and Johnny Lee to compile their own lists. We asked Dolly Parton, Rosanne Cash and Rodney Dillard about the worst shows they'd ever played, got Chris LeDoux to write about the wildest horses he'd ever ridden and even talked Don Williams and Tom T. Hall into supplying some of their favorite recipes.

But things didn't stop there. We also went to Country music fans in various parts of the world and talked to them about their particular heroes. And we sought to answer many of the questions that came our way by providing a comprehensive fan club directory along with a listing of contact addresses for many of Country's leading entertainers.

The result is a book that is both useful and entertaining. One that you can dip into for oddball facts while queueing to see Tammy. One that you can also keep in a handy position on your bookshelf as a source of reference about bestselling and rare records, poll-winning acts and scores of other things most Country buffs always need to know.

A lot of love and a lot of fun went into putting it all together. We hope it shows.

Fred Richard

Fred Dellar and Richard Wootton

AM I THAT EASY TO FORGET?

Great song titles of our time and the folk who brought them into our lives

Jimmy Buffett	*My Head Hurts, My Feet Stink And I Don't Love Jesus*
Little Jimmy Dickens	*May The Bird of Paradise Fly Up Your Nose*
The Bellamy Brothers	*If I Said You Had A Beautiful Body, Would You Hold It Against Me?*
Shel Silverstein	*Sahra Cynthia Sylvia Stout Would Not Take The Garbage Out*
Rex Allen	*Jose Villa Lobo Alfredo Thomoso Vincente Lopez*
Dallas Frazier	*Common, Broke Elastic, Rotten Cotton, Funky Fuzzy, White Sock Blues No.2*
Don Reno and Red Smiley	*Your Tears Are Just Interest On The Loan*
Homer and Jethro	*Jam Bowl Liar*
Chick and The Hot Rods	*Jimmy Caught The Dickens, Pushing Ernest In The Tubb*
Roy Drusky	*Peel Me A Nanner*
Dave Kirby	*Her And Her Car And Her Mobile Home*
Roger Miller	*You Can't Roller Skate In A Buffalo Herd*
Joanna Neel	*Daddy Was A Preacher But Mama Was A Go-Go Girl*
Norma Jean	*Don't Let That Doorknob Hit You*
Johnny Paycheck	*Don't Monkey With Another Monkey's Monkey*
Statler Brothers	*You Can't Have Your Kate And Edith Too*
Ernest Tubb	*It's For God And Country And You Mom*
Tex Williams	*The Night Miss Nancy Ann's Hotel For Single Girls Burned Down*
Mac Wiseman	*Johnny's Cash And Charley's Pride*
Johnny Bond	*Hot Rod Surfin' Hootlebeatnanny*
Brush Arbor	*Folk, Rock, Pop, Middle Of The Road Country Singer*
Connie Cato	*Who Wants A Slightly Used Woman?*
Dave Dudley	*Rolaids, Doan's Pills And Preparation H*

George Jones and Johnny Paycheck	*When You're Ugly Like Us, You Just Naturally Got To Be Cool*
Marty Robbins	*One Man's Trash Is Another Man's Treasure*
L.E. White and Lola Jean Dillon	*You're The Reason Our Kids Are Ugly*
Hoyt Axton	*You're The Hangnail In My Life*
Roy Clark	*The Laurence Welk, Hee Haw, Counter-Revolution Polka*
Roger Miller	*My Uncle Used To Love Me But She Died*
Grandpa Jones	*I'm Tying The Leaves So They Won't Come Down*
Little David Wilkins	*Who Ever Turned You On Forgot to Turn You Off*
Cal Smith	*Between Lust And Watching TV*
Carson Robinson	*Store Bought Teeth*
Homer and Jethro	*There Ain't A Chicken Safe In Tennessee*
Bobby Bare	*Your Credit Card Won't Get You Into Heaven*
Billy Edd Wheeler	*The Interstate Is Coming Through My Outhouse*

Jimmy Buffett

AMONG MY SOUVENIRS

Souvenir shops and fan-orientated businesses

Several Country stars have shops, museums and other fan-orientated businesses, which they either own or have named after them, in the Nashville area. Here is a selection:

Willie Nelson & Family General Store
915 North Gallatin Road,
Madison, Tennessee
(Tel: 615 865 6099)

There's no admission charge to this shop, which is run by Frank and Jeanie Oakley, who've known Willie Nelson for over 15 years. There are numerous souvenirs plus "Willie's Picture Gallery" and the "Wall Of Fame."

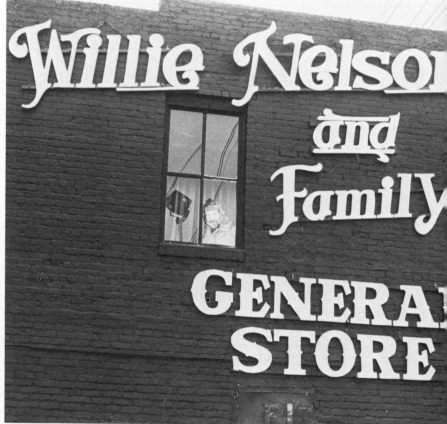

House of Cash
700 East Main Street,
Hendersonville, Tennessee
(Tel: 615 824 5110)

Twitty City
(directly across from the House of Cash)
1 Music Village Blvd,
Hendersonville, Tennessee
(Tel: 615 822 6650)

Conway Twitty's Country Store & Record Shop
1530 Demonbreum Street,
Nashville, Tennessee
(Tel: 615 256 8299)

The Johnny Cash museum is open to the public and there's a souvenir shop where you can purchase antiques and jewelry collected by June Carter Cash.
Open Monday through Saturday, 9 a.m. to 4.30 p.m.

Built in the grounds of Conway Twitty's house and those of his children, includes "Conway's Showcase," a multi-media entertainment experience which traces Conway's life and career. The Twitty City Gift Shop features a complete line in Twitty souvenirs.
Open daily, May 1 through Labor Day 9 a.m. to 9 p.m., September through April 9 a.m. to 5 p.m.

Well-stocked record store that's particularly useful if you're looking for singles; also sells numerous Country gifts.

Left: Willie Nelson's store and its policy

Right: Welcome sign outside Twitty City and *below:* not-so-welcome sign outside the House of Cash

Alabama Band Gifts and Souvenirs
118 16th Avenue South,
Nashville, Tennessee

A wide range of Alabama souvenirs plus Nashville specialty items – like GooGoo Bars.
Open from 9 a.m. to 9 p.m.

Hank Williams Jr General Store
(across from the Hall of Fame Museum)
Demonbreum Street,
Nashville, Tennessee

Wide range of souvenirs, including the famous Hank and baby Hank coffee cup, tour jackets, belt buckles and records.

Ernest Tubb Record Shops
(two locations)
417 Broadway, Nashville and
Music Valley Drive
(Tel: 615 255 7503)

The shop in Nashville's Broadway is across from the Ryman Auditorium, the home of the Grand Ole Opry for many years. The shop has a large stock and offers a mail order service: PO Box 500, Nashville, Tennessee 37202, USA. The new location across from the Opryland Hotel is the site of "The Midnight Jamboree," a live radio show broadcast every Saturday night, after the Opry, on WSM-AM.

Roy Acuff Museum
(at Opryland)
2802 Opryland Drive,
Nashville, Tennessee
(Tel: 615 889 6611)

Roy Acuff began collecting antique guns in the early forties, then began collecting hand-painted ties, musical instruments and whatever interested him on his travels. His museum is now located inside Opryland and concentrates on music and musical instruments.

Jim Reeves Museum
Gallatin Road,
(south at Briley Parkway)
Nashville, Tennessee
(Tel: 615 266 2065)

Located in Evergreen Place, a manor house built in 1794, the museum contains many souvenirs of Jim Reeves' world-wide success, including his original tour bus and equipment from the radio station where he worked as a disc jockey, put together with great care by his widow, Mary Reeves.

Barbara Mandrell's One Hour Photo
1522 Demonbreum Street,
Nashville, Tennessee
(and three other locations)

Perhaps the most functional fan-orientated business in Nashville, Barbara's fast-service stores also sell Mandrell Sisters' souvenir items.

Boots Randolph's
209 Printers Alley,
Nashville, Tennessee
(Tel: 615 256 5500)

Popular night spot that features regular appearances by saxophonist Boots Randolph. Steak and Alaskan king crab legs the house specialty!

Loretta Lynn's Dude Ranch
Hurricane Mills, Tennessee
(some 64 miles from Nashville)
(Tel: 615 296 7700)

Located in the tiny town of Hurricane Mills, which Loretta owns, the ranch offers camping facilities, riding stables, canoe rentals, a miniature golf course, rodeos, live campfire shows, Loretta Lynn's museum, a general store and much more.
Open April through October.

AND THE BAND PLAYED WALTZING MATILDA

Country down-under

This list of the all-time Australasian Country music recorded greats was compiled for the *Country Music Annual* (BAL Marketing) with the assistance of Eddie Birt, Hedley Charles, Eric Watson and John Minson. Records are not in order of importance.

Tex Morton	*The Black Sheep*
Slim Dusty	*Pub With No Beer*
Chad Morgan	*The Sheik From Scrubby Creek*
Buddy Williams	*Where The White-Faced Cattle Roam*
Smoky Dawson	*My Heart Is Where The Roper Flows Tonight*
Slim Dusty	*When The Rain Tumbles Down In July*
Shirley Thoms	*Where The Golden Wattle Blooms*
Slim Newton	*Redback On The Toilet Seat*
Johnny Ashcroft	*Little Boy Lost*
Kevin Shegog	*One Small Photograph*
Reg Lindsay	*Armstrong*
Hawking Brothers	*One Day At A Time*
Lucky Starr	*I've Been Everywhere*
Jimmy Little	*Royal Telephone*
Buddy Williams	*Heading For The Warwick Rodeo*
Slim Dusty	*Trumby*
Reg Lindsay	*Sulva Bay*
Singing Kettles	*Toy Telephone*
Johnny Ashcroft	*And The Band Played Waltzing Matilda*
Tex Morton	*The Goondiwindi Grey*
McKean Sisters	*Gymkhana Yodel*
Tim McNamara	*Going To The Rodeo*
Webb Brothers	*Call Of The Bellbird*

Slim Dusty/Barry Thornton	*Winter Winds*
Buddy Williams	*Music In My Pony's Feet*
Tex Morton	*Mandrake*
Gordon Parsons	*Where The Bellinger River Flows*
Rick and Thel Carey	*You Can Say That Again*
Billy Starlight	*The Red Morning Sun*
Kevin King	*Rub-A-Dub-Dub*
Eddie Tapp	*Star Of Love*
Slim Dusty	*Lights On The Hill*
Gordon Parsons	*The Passing Of Cobber Jack*
Saltbush	*Annie Johnson*
Slim Dusty	*Camooweal*
Peter Posa	*White Rabbit*
Trevor Day	*Boy Soldier*
Buddy Bishop	*Farmyard Yodel*
Tex Morton	*The Transport Man*
Reg Lindsay	*Down In The Well*
Slim Dusty	*Walk a Country Mile*
Reg Poole	*Goin' Rodeoin'*
Eddie Tapp	*My Father's Voice*
Slim Dusty	*Duncan*

Slim Dusty

COMMERCIAL AFFECTION

Country Music advertising

Country music has been used to sell things since the earliest days. The Grand Ole Opry was launched on a Nashville radio station in the twenties for the sole purpose of selling insurance to working people in the American South, while several Country entertainers, including a very young Roy Acuff, were hired by traveling medicine shows to attract an audience with their singing before the serious business of selling medicinal compounds. In the eighties, advertisers, particularly of beer and fast food, have found that sales can be improved significantly with the use of a Country star or two. This list was compiled by the Country Music Association in Nashville.

Alabama	*Dr Pepper*
Rex Allen Jr	*Ford Farm Tractors, Carrier Air Conditioning*
Bill Anderson	*Po Folks Restaurants*
Lynn Anderson	*Nabisco Country Crackers*
Hoyt Axton	*Busch Beer*
Moe Bandy	*Miller Beer, Eureka Log Homes*
Bellamy Brothers	*Miller Beer*
Debby Boone	*Leggs*
Jim Ed Brown	*Dollar General Stores*
Ed Bruce	*Big Duke Chewing Tobacco*
Roy Clark	*Wyler's Lemonade*
Jerry Clower	*Little General Convenience Stores, Ambush Sutherland Corporations*
Helen Cornelius	*United States Marine Corps*
Charlie Daniels	*Skoal, Busch Beer*
Freddy Fender	*McDonald's (in Spanish)*
Tennessee Ernie Ford	*Martha White Foods*
Janie Fricke	*Budweiser Beer, United Airlines, Red Lobster, Tuesday's*
Larry Gatlin and The Gatlin Brothers	*Kentucky Fried Chicken, American Express*
Crystal Gayle	*Avon*
Mickey Gilley	*Schlitz Beer*

Hager Brothers	*J.C. Penney*
Tom T. Hall	*Chevrolet Pickup Trucks, Tyson Foods*
Wendy Holcombe	*Purina Dog Chow*
Grandpa Jones	*Clifty Farms*
Kendalls	*Shure Instruments*
Johnny Lee	*Schlitz Beer*
Loretta Lynn	*Crisco, Allis-Chalmers Farm Equipment*
Roger Miller	*General Foods Mellow Roast Coffee, AT&T*
Minnie Pearl	*Spic and Span, American Egg Board*
Anne Murray	*Canadian Imperial Bank of Commerce*
Jimmy C. Newman	*Clifty Farms*
Oak Ridge Boys	*AT&T, Boy Scouts of America*
Sandy Powell	*Nocona Boots*
Charley Pride	*Country Pride Chicken*
Eddie Rabbitt	*Miller Beer*
Jerry Reed	*Laredo, Truckstops of America, Mercury Motors*
Charlie Rich	*Dr Pepper*
Jeannie C. Riley	*Purina Pet Foods*

Jerry Reed

: Loretta Lynn, grand-
…ter Beth-Anne Lyle,
…ter Sissy and husband
…ey in a 'Crisco' TV
…t

Johnny Rodriguez	*Amalie Oil*
T.G. Sheppard	*Shure Instruments, IRS, Budweiser Beer*
Statler Brothers	*Kraft Miracle Margarine*
Sylvia	*Durango Boots*
Ray Stevens	*Flavorich*
Nat Stuckey	*United Airlines, Esco Mining, Slim Jims*
Mel Tillis	*What-A-Burger, Fina Gas Company*
Hank Williams, Jr	*AT&T*
Tammy Wynette	*McDonald's*

Right: Mickey Gilley and Johnny Lee toast each other with Schlitz Beer

Below: Bill Anderson had a hit with a song about 'Po Folks' and now advertises similarly named restaurants

THE COUNTRY MUSIC HALL OF FAME

Hall of Fame members

The Country Music Hall of Fame was founded in 1961 by the Country Music Association in Nashville and honors both performers and industry figures who have made special contributions to Country music. Hall of Fame inductees are selected each year by a panel of 200 electors, consisting of people who've been active participants in the music business for at least fifteen years. The electors vote by secret ballot and the winners are traditionally announced on the CMA Awards show in October. Hall of Fame plaques are displayed at the Country Music Hall of Fame and Museum at 4 Music Square East, Nashville, Tennessee. Beside the plaques are portraits and display cases, which contain museum objects which relate to each person's career.

Jimmie Rodgers
September 8, 1897–May 26, 1933
(elected 1961)

Jimmie Rodgers (James Charles Rodgers), "The Singing Brakeman," "The Mississippi Blue Yodeller," had a very short but successful career, dying of TB at the age of 35 but leaving a legacy of songs that was to have a profound influence on future performers. His plaque reads, "Jimmie Rodgers' name stands foremost in the country music field as 'the man who started it all'." He was the obvious first choice for the Hall of Fame.

Fred Rose
August 24, 1897–December 1, 1954
(elected 1961)

One of the most important back-room figures in Country music history, Fred Rose was a very successful publisher; he started the Acuff-Rose publishing house with singer Roy Acuff. He was a gifted songwriter, and played a vital role in the career development of many up-and-coming stars, including Hank Williams.

Hank Williams
September 17, 1923–January 1, 1953
(elected 1961)

Hank Williams (Hiram King Williams), "The Drifting Cowboy," the first superstar of Country music, a brilliant songwriter and an unforgettable performer, who died at the age of 29 after a troubled and frequently unhappy life. He deserves particular credit for opening up Country music to a wider audience: several of his best songs became huge pop hits for other entertainers.

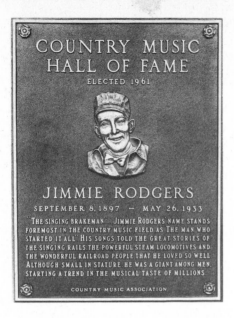

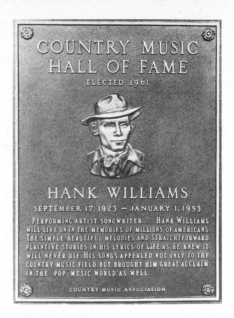

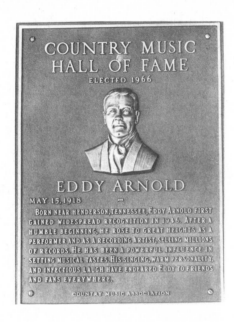

Roy Acuff
September 15, 1903–
(elected 1962)

Roy Acuff, "The Smokey Mountain Boy," "The King Of Country Music", became the first living person to be elected to the Hall of Fame. The Country entertainer most closely associated with the Grand Ole Opry, Roy has been a regular and popular performer on the show since the late thirties.

Tex Ritter
January 12, 1907–January 2, 1974
(elected 1964)

Tex Ritter (Woodward Maurice Ritter) was a popular and versatile Country and Western entertainer; a star of radio, television, films, the Broadway stage and records. His hits included the theme song from the movie *High Noon*.

Ernest Tubb
February 9, 1914–
(elected 1965)

Ernest Tubb, "The Texas Troubadour," one of Country music's best-loved early stars, has been making records for over forty years and his biggest hit was "Walking The Floor Over You." His long career was inspired by Jimmie Rodgers, his hero since childhood.

Eddy Arnold
May 15, 1918–
(elected 1966)

Eddy Arnold (Richard Edward Arnold), "The Tennessee Plowboy," was one of the first Country-pop crossover artists and the bestselling Country singer in America after the death of Hank Williams and until the late sixties.

James R. Denny
February 28, 1911–August 27, 1963
(elected 1966)

Jim Denny was a leader in Country music publishing (he formed the giant Cedarwood company), management (the Jim Denny Artist Bureau) and radio (WSM and the Grand Ole Opry). His plaque notes that "He served to promote, protect and encourage some of the most important artists in the industry."

George D. Hay
November 9, 1895–May 8, 1968
(elected 1966)

The self-styled "Solemn Old Judge" who introduced the very first WSM Barn Dance, the Saturday night radio show which became the Grand Ole Opry. He continued to act as master of ceremonies for nearly thirty years.

Uncle Dave Macon
October 7, 1870–March 22, 1952
(elected 1966)

Uncle Dave Macon (David Harrison Macon), "The Dixie Dewdrop," the first star of Country music: he sang old-time ballads, played the banjo and was a regular and popular performer on the Grand Ole Opry from 1926 until his retirement (at the age of 82) in 1952.

Red Foley
June 17, 1910–September 19, 1968
(elected 1967)

Red Foley (Clyde Julian Foley) was the versatile star of three of the most popular radio barn dance shows – the Chicago-based National Barn Dance, the Renfro Valley Barn Dance and the Grand Ole Opry – and one of the earliest Country music TV shows – Ozark Jubilee.

J.L. (Joe) Frank
April 15, 1900–May 4, 1952
(elected 1967)

Joe Frank was an early Country music promoter who did much to help the careers of Gene Autry, Roy Acuff, Pee Wee King, Eddy Arnold, Minnie Pearl, and Ernest Tubb.

Jim Reeves
August 20, 1924–July 31, 1964
(elected 1967)

"Gentleman" Jim Reeves was one of the most internationally popular stars of Country music. He died tragically in a 'plane crash in 1964 but continued to have bestselling records for many years because of the large amount of previously unreleased material that he left behind.

Stephen S. Sholes
February 12, 1911–April 22, 1968
(elected 1967)

Steve Sholes was an RCA executive who played a key role in the growth of the Country music industry – he established the first major record company offices in Nashville and "discovered" several major stars, including Eddy Arnold, Chet Atkins and Jim Reeves. He was responsible for the signing of Elvis Presley.

Bob Wills
March 6, 1905–May 13, 1975
(elected 1968)

Bob Wills, "The King Of Western Swing," the fiddle-playing, wisecracking leader of the Texas Playboys, the most popular of the Western Swing bands of the thirties and forties. He made hundreds of records in his 44-year career, including bestselling "San Antonio Rose."

Gene Autry
September 29, 1907–
(elected 1969)

One of the first and most popular of the singing cowboys, Gene Autry had many big-selling records, including "Silver Haired Daddy Of Mine" and "Rudolph The Red-Nosed Reindeer," and appeared in countless cowboy films, invariably with his famous horse Champion.

Bill Monroe
September 13, 1911–
(elected 1970)

Bill Monroe (William Smith Monroe), the mandolin-playing "Father of Bluegrass" who developed and perfected the genre, influencing generations of young musicians. His best-known compositions include "Uncle Pen" and "Blue Moon Of Kentucky."

The Original Carter Family
A.P. Carter December 15, 1891–
November 7, 1960
Maybelle Carter May 10, 1909–
October 23, 1978
Sara Carter July 21, 1899–January
8, 1979
(elected 1970)

A.P. Carter, his wife Sara, and his sister-in-law Maybelle were featured on one of the very first commercial Country music recording sessions, at Bristol, Tennessee in August 1927, and subsequently became one of the most popular and influential of the early Country groups.

Arthur Edward Satherley
October 19, 1889–
(elected 1971)

The first English-born member of the Hall of Fame, Arthur Satherley, "Uncle Art," played a significant role in the early days of the American recording industry and was talent scout for ARC, and later CBS, "discovering" Roy Acuff, Bob Wills and Gene Autry, among others.

Jimmie H. Davis
September 11, 1902–
(elected 1972)

Country singer, songwriter and public servant – Jimmie Davis was twice elected Governor of Louisiana – he's best known for the hit song "You Are My Sunshine."

Chet Atkins
June 20, 1924–
(elected 1973)

Chet Atkins (Chester Burton Atkins), "Mr Guitar," a gifted and influential guitarist, record company executive and producer – for RCA – from the mid-fifties until 1979. He played an important part in the successful careers of RCA stars, including Charley Pride, Jim Reeves, Jerry Reed, Don Gibson and Elvis Presley.

Patsy Cline
September 8, 1932–March 5, 1963
(elected 1973)

Patsy Cline (Virginia Patterson Hensley) was one of the greatest female vocalists in Country music but her career was cut tragically short when she was killed in a 'plane crash in 1963. She's best remembered for the recordings of "Crazy" and "I Fall To Pieces."

Owen Bradley
October 21, 1915–
(elected 1974)

A pioneer of the famed "Nashville Sound" in the late fifties, Owen Bradley was head of Decca Records for many years and produced most of the label's top acts, including Ernest Tubb, Patsy Cline, Red Foley, Brenda Lee and Loretta Lynn.

Frank "Pee Wee" King
February 18, 1914–
(elected 1974)

Accordion- and fiddle-playing bandleader who made many records and appeared in several films and countless radio and TV broadcasts. He also had considerable success as a songwriter, co-authoring "Bonaparte's Retreat" and "Tennessee Waltz" among others.

Minnie Pearl
October 25, 1912–
(elected 1975)

Minnie Pearl (Sarah Ophelia Colley), the Country humorist best known for her dimestore hat with the dangling price tag and the catch phrase, "How-dee! I'm just so proud to be here," has been a star of the Grand Ole Opry for over forty years.

Paul Cohen
November 10, 1908–April 1, 1971
(elected 1976)

Paul Cohen was one of the first people to recognize the potential of Nashville as a recording centre. He opened the first recording studio in the city, for Decca, in 1945, hired Owen Bradley and helped the budding careers of Decca stars like Kitty Wells, Ernest Tubb, Red Foley, Webb Pierce and Patsy Cline.

Kitty Wells
August 30, 1919–
(elected 1976)

Kitty Wells (Muriel Deason), known as "The Queen of Country Music," began her long hit-making career with "It Wasn't God Who Made Honky Tonk Angels" in 1952.

Merle Travis
November 29, 1917–October 20, 1983
(elected 1977)

Merle Travis was a multi-talented guitarist, singer, songwriter, actor and cartoonist who won widespread popularity on radio, record, stage, film and TV in a career that lasted over forty years. His most successful records include "Divorce Me COD," and his best-known song is "Sixteen Tons," which he co-authored with Tennessee Ernie Ford.

Grandpa Jones
October 20, 1913–
(elected 1978)

Grandpa Jones (Louis Marshall Jones) is another long-established Country music all-rounder – singer, songwriter, banjo and guitar player, and comedian. A "Grandpa" since his early twenties, Jones is a popular and regular performer on the Grand Ole Opry and the "Hee Haw" TV show.

Hank Snow
May 9, 1914–
(elected 1979)

Hank Snow (Clarence Eugene Snow) is one of the best-known Country stars. A gifted singer, songwriter and guitarist, Canadian-born Hank has been a regular on the Grand Ole Opry since 1950, and his long recording career, including a record-breaking forty-five years with RCA, has yielded many hits, most notably "I'm Movin' On."

Hubert Long
December 3, 1923–September 7, 1972
(elected 1979)

Hubert Long opened Nashville's first talent agency, in 1953, and subsequently helped the careers of many stars, including Bill Anderson, George Jones, Ferlin Husky, Skeeter Davis and David Houston.

Johnny Cash
February 26, 1932–
(elected 1980)

The best-known and most widely traveled Country entertainer in the world is John R. Cash, the "Man In Black," whose career began in the same small Memphis studio as Elvis Presley, Carl Perkins and Jerry Lee Lewis.

Connie B. Gay
August 22, 1914–
(elected 1980)

Connie B. Gay has been an important force and guiding light in modern Country music. His Hall of Fame plaque notes that "His pioneer use of the term 'country music' and registered trademark 'Town and Country' were instrumental in bringing Country music 'uptown'."

Original Sons Of The Pioneers
Hugh Farr December 6, 1903–
March 17, 1980
Karl Farr April 29, 1909–
September 20, 1961
Bob Nolan April 1, 1908–June 15, 1980
Lloyd Perryman January 29, 1917–
May 31, 1977
Roy Rogers November 5, 1911–
Tim Spencer July 13, 1908–April 26, 1974
(elected 1980)

The Sons Of The Pioneers were the originators and finest exponents of western harmony. They formed in 1933, made many records, including "Tumbling Tumbleweeds" and "Cool Water," and appeared in numerous films, often with founder member Roy Rogers, who left in the late thirties to pursue an acting career as "King Of The Cowboys."

Vernon Dalhart
April 6, 1883–September 14, 1948
(elected 1981)

Vernon Dalhart (Marion Try Slaughter) recorded Country music's first million seller – "The Prisoner's Song" c/w "The Wreck Of The Old 97." He made an enormous number of records, used over one hundred different names and sang in a variety of styles, from Country to opera.

Grant Turner
May 17, 1912–
(elected 1981)

Grant Turner was the protégé of George D. Hay and began master of ceremonies duties at the Opry in 1945. He's now revered as the "Dean of Opry Announcers."

Lefty Frizzell
March 31, 1928–July 19, 1975
(elected 1982)

Lefty Frizzell (William Orville Frizzell) was a boxer for a while, hence the nickname (which came from his strong left hook). He became a Country star in the fifties and sixties, scoring numerous hits including "Always Late," "If You've Got The Money, I've Got The Time" and "I Love You In A Thousand Ways."

Roy Horton
November 5, 1914–
(elected 1982)

Roy Horton was one of Country music's most versatile recording specialists before becoming a top music publishing executive with the Peer-Southern organization.

Marty Robbins
September 26, 1925–December 8, 1982
(elected 1982)

Marty Robbins was one of Country music's best-loved and most successful stars. He began scoring hits in 1953, had several crossover-pop successes, including "El Paso" and "A White Sports Coat," and was still a Country chart regular when he died, in 1982.

Little Jimmy Dickens
December 19, 1925–
(elected 1983)

Affectionately known as "Tater," Little Jimmy, who's under five feet in height, claims to be the first Country singer to circle the globe on a world tour. A hitmaker in the '40s, he scored his biggest success with "May The Bird Of Paradise Fly Up Your Nose" in 1965.

DRIFT AWAY

Desert island fantasies

We asked a number of Country entertainers to imagine that they were cast adrift on a desert island and to choose the five or six people they would like to take with them.

Janie Fricke

My husband, *Randy Jackson*, who's my manager, my friend and a very dear person.

My mother, *Phyllis Fricke*, because she's very dear to me.

My sister, because we could sing together. We started singing together.

Then I'd take Randy's mother, *Floreine Jackson*, who's a great lady and also the President of my fan club.

President Reagan, because I've sung for him a couple of times and he reminds me of my daddy a little bit and he just seemed like a really nice person when I met him.

Janie Fricke

Lee Greenwood

Lee Greenwood

My wife, *Melanie*, for obvious reasons; she's a beautiful lady and I love her very much. She's also very talented and knows about my profession, and it would be nice to be able to discuss my profession with somebody.

Larry McFaden, my manager and my friend: we have a lot of fun together.

My four children, *Mark, Ted, Laura* and *Kelly*.

Johnny Carson, then I could have my interviews when I wanted them!

George Jones – I'd like to have him where I can at least see him perform once in a while. There'd be a pretty good chance that he'd show up too!

Brenda Lee

Brenda Lee

My husband, *Ronnie Shacklett*, because for the past twenty years I've spent about all my life with him, since I was eighteen years old, and he's been my strength and my anchor. If I'm going to be marooned on a desert island I'm going to need a lot of strength.

My two daughters, *Julie* and *Jolie*, I can't go for two days without seeing them, much less two years.

Ann Landers, because she would have the answers to any problems that might arise.

Irma Bombeck – she's on the "Good Morning America" TV show and she's a marvelous person, one of the funniest people around. She talks about life and all our quirks and makes them seem wonderful. Her talent to amuse would probably make the time fly by.

Loretta Lynn – there are lots of great singers that I'd love to take with me; if Mahalia Jackson was still alive I'd take her, but I'll settle for Loretta because I love her.

Joe Bonsall of the
Oak Ridge Boys

My wife, *Mary*, because I can't survive five days without her, so I couldn't survive two or three years.

My daughter, *Jennifer*, and my stepdaughter, *Sabrina*.

Mike Schmitt – he's third-base with the Philadelphia Phillies and I'd love to talk baseball with him.

Neil Diamond – musically, I'd like to have cassettes from everyone from Merle Haggard to John Anderson, but if I had to choose one music business person, I guess I'd go for Neil.

Richard Sterban of the
Oak Ridge Boys

My three sons, *Richie*, *Doug* and *Christopher*.

Sheena Easton, because she's my favorite singer.

Morgan Fairchild (actress from the TV show "Flamingo Road"), because I like the way she looks.

Joe Necrow of the Houston Astros, one of the best friends the Oak Ridge Boys have in the major leagues. After music, baseball is our second love.

Reba McEntire

Charlie, my husband and best buddy, because we get along real well.

Mommy, because we love to gossip.

Daddy, because he'll line us up and keep us straight.

Susie, my little sister. She used to travel with me and sing in my group.

Little Jake, he's my nephew and the reason Susie had to quit touring with me. Susie stays at home with him now, looks after the books for me and looks after the house.

Reba McEntire

ENGLAND SWINGS

British Top Twenty successes by US Country stars . . .

Lynn Anderson	*Rose Garden* (CBS)	**1971**	(3)
Eddy Arnold	*Make The World Go Away* (RCA)	**1966**	(6)
J.J. Barrie	*No Charge* (Power Exchange)	**1976**	(1)
Bellamy Brothers	*Let Your Love Flow* (Warner Bros)	**1976**	(7)
	If I Said You Had A Beautiful Body (Warner Bros)	**1979**	(3)
Glen Campbell	*Wichita Lineman* (Ember)	**1969**	(7)
	Galveston (Ember)	**1969**	(14)
	Honey Come Back (Capitol)	**1970**	(4)
	It's Only Make Believe (Capitol)	**1970**	(4)
	Rhinestone Cowboy (Capitol)	**1975**	(4)
Johnny Cash	*A Boy Named Sue* (CBS)	**1969**	(4)
	A Thing Called Love (CBS)	**1972**	(4)
Floyd Cramer	*On The Rebound* (RCA)	**1961**	(1)
Charlie Daniels Band	*The Devil Went Down To Georgia* (Epic)	**1979**	(14)
Skeeter Davis	*End Of The World* (RCA)	**1963**	(18)
Jimmy Dean	*Big Bad John* Philips)	**1961**	(2)
Deliverance Soundtrack (actually Eric Weissberg and Steve Mandell	*Duelling Banjos* (Warner Bros)	**1973**	(17)
John Denver	*Annie's Song* (RCA)	**1974**	(1)
Johnny Duncan and The Blue Grass Boys	*Last Train To San Fernando* (Columbia)	**1957**	(2)

Glen Campbell (*right*)

Everly Brothers	*Bye Bye Love* (London)	**1957**	(6)
	Wake Up Little Susie (London)	**1957**	(2)
	All I Have To Do Is Dream (London)	**1958**	(1)
	Bird Dog (London)	**1958**	(2)
	Problems (London)	**1959**	(6)
	Poor Jenny (London)	**1959**	(14)
	Take A Message To Mary (London)	**1959**	(20)
	('Til) I Kissed You (London)	**1959**	(2)
	Let It Be Me (London)	**1960**	(13)
	Cathy's Clown (Warner Bros)	**1960**	(1)
	When Will I Be Loved (London)	**1960**	(4)
	Lucille (Warner Bros)	**1960**	(4)
	Like Strangers (London)	**1960**	(11)
	Walk Right Back (Warner Bros)	**1961**	(1)
	Temptation (Warner Bros)	**1961**	(1)
	Muskrat (Warner Bros)	**1961**	(6)
	Cryin' In The Rain (Warner Bros)	**1962**	(6)
	How Can I Meet Her (Warner Bros)	**1962**	(12)
	No One Can Make My Sunshine Smile (Warner Bros)	**1962**	(11)
	The Price Of Love (Warner Bros)	**1965**	(2)
	Love Is Strange (Warner Bros)	**1965**	(11)
Tennessee Ernie Ford	*Give Me Your Word* (Capitol)	**1955**	(1)
	Sixteen Tons (Capitol)	**1956**	(1)
	The Ballad Of Davy Crockett (Capitol)	**1956**	(3)
Crystal Gayle	*Don't It Make My Brown Eyes Blue* (United Artists)	**1977**	(5)
	Talking In Your Sleep (United Artists)	**1978**	(11)
Bobbie Gentry	*Ode To Billie Joe* (Capitol)	**1967**	(13)
	I'll Never Fall In Love Again (Capitol)	**1969**	(1)
Bobby Gentry and Glen Campbell	*All I Have To Do Is Dream* (Capitol)	**1969**	(3)
Don Gibson	*Sea Of Heartbreak* (RCA)	**1961**	(14)
Bobby Helms	*Jacqueline* (Brunswick)	**1958**	(20)
Johnny Horton	*Battle Of New Orleans* (Philips)	**1959**	(16)
Burl Ives	*A Little Bitty Tear* (Brunswick)	**1962**	(9)
Sonny James	*Young Love* (Capitol)	**1957**	(11)
Bill Justis	*Raunchy* (London)	**1958**	(11)
Brenda Lee	*Sweet Nuthings* (Brunswick)	**1960**	(4)
	I'm Sorry (Brunswick)	**1960**	(12)
	Let's Jump The Broomstick (Brunswick)	**1961**	(12)
	Speak To Me Pretty (Brunswick)	**1962**	(3)
	Here Comes That Feeling (Brunswick)	**1962**	(5)
	It Started All Over Again (Brunswick)	**1962**	(15)
	Rockin' Around The Christmas Tree (Brunswick)	**1962**	(6)
	All Alone Am I (Brunswick)	**1963**	(7)
	Losing You (Brunswick)	**1963**	(10)
	I Wonder (Brunswick)	**1963**	(14)

	As Usual (Brunswick)	**1964**	(5)
	Is It True? (Brunswick)	**1964**	(17)
Jerry Lee Lewis	*Whole Lotta Shakin' Goin' On* (London)	**1957**	(8)
	Great Balls Of Fire (London)	**1957**	(1)
	Breathless (London)	**1958**	(8)
	High School Confidential (London)	**1959**	(12)
	What'd I Say? (London)	**1961**	(10)
Hank Locklin	*Please Help Me, I'm Falling* (RCA)	**1960**	(9)
	We're Gonna Go Fishin' (RCA)	**1962**	(18)
Bonnie Lou	*Tennessee Wig Walk* (Parlophone)	**1954**	(4)
John D. Loudermilk	*The Language Of Love* (RCA)	**1962**	(13)
Jim Lowe	*Green Door* (London)	**1956**	(8)
Bob Luman	*Let's Think About Living* (Warner Bros)	**1960**	(6)
C.W. McCall	*Convoy* (MGM)	**1976**	(2)
Wink Martindale	*A Deck Of Cards* (London)	**1959**	(18)
	A Deck Of Cards (London)	**1963**	(5)
Ned Miller	*From A Jack To A King* (London)	**1963**	(2)
Roger Miller	*King Of The Road* (Philips)	**1965**	(1)
	England Swings (Philips)	**1965**	(13)
	Little Green Apples (Mercury)	**1968**	(19)
Rick Nelson	*Poor Little Fool* (London)	**1958**	(4)
	Someday (London)	**1958**	(9)
	It's Late (London)	**1959**	(3)
	Never Be Anyone Else But You (London)	**1959**	(14)
	Sweeter Than You (London)	**1959**	(19)
	Just A Little Too Much (London)	**1959**	(11)
	Hello Mary Lou (London)	**1961**	(2)
	Young World (London)	**1962**	(19)
	Fools Rush In (Brunswick)	**1963**	(12)
	For You (Brunswick)	**1964**	(14)
Dolly Parton	*Jolene* (RCA)	**1976**	(7)
Carl Perkins	*Blue Suede Shoes* (London)	**1956**	(10)
Marvin Rainwater	*Whole Lotta Woman* (MGM)	**1958**	(1)
	I Dig You Baby (MGM)	**1958**	(19)
Jim Reeves	*He'll Have To Go* (RCA)	**1960**	(12)
	You're The Only Good Thing (RCA)	**1961**	(17)
	Welcome To My World (RCA)	**1962**	(6)
	I Love You Because (RCA)	**1964**	(5)
	I Won't Forget You (RCA)	**1964**	(3)
	There's A Heartache Following Me (RCA)	**1964**	(6)
	It Hurts So Much (RCA)	**1965**	(8)
	Not Until The Next Time (RCA)	**1965**	(13)
	Is It Really Over? (RCA)	**1965**	(17)
	Distant Drums (RCA)	**1966**	(1)

	I Won't Come In While He's There (RCA)	**1967**	(12)
	When Two World Collide (RCA)	**1969**	(17)
	But You Love Me Daddy (RCA)	**1969**	(15)
Charlie Rich	*The Most Beautiful Girl* (CBS)	**1974**	(2)
	Behind Closed Doors (Epic)	**1974**	(16)
Jeannie C. Riley	*Harper Valley PTA* (Polydor)	**1968**	(12)
Tex Ritter	*The Wayward Wind* (Capitol)	**1956**	(8)
Marty Robbins	*El Paso* (Fontana)	**1960**	(19)
	Devil Woman (CBS)	**1962**	(5)
Kenny Rogers	*Ruby Don't Take Your Love To Town* (Reprise)	**1969**	(2)
	Something's Burning (Reprise)	**1970**	(8)
	Lucille (United Artists)	**1977**	(1)
	Coward Of The County (United Artists)	**1980**	(1)
	Lady (Liberty)	**1980**	(12)
Kenny Rogers and Dolly Parton	*Islands In The Stream* (RCA)	**1984**	(7)
Red Sovine	*Teddy Bear* (Starday)	**1981**	(4)
Billie Jo Spears	*Blanket On The Ground* (United Artists)	**1975**	(6)
	What I've Got In Mind (United Artists)	**1976**	(4)
Jim Stafford	*Spiders And Snakes* (MGM)	**1974**	(14)
	My Girl Bill (MGM)	**1974**	(20)
Starland Vocal Band	*Afternoon Delight* (RCA)	**1976**	(18)
Ray Stevens	*Everything Is Beautiful* (CBS)	**1970**	(6)
	Bridget The Midget (CBS)	**1971**	(2)
	The Streak (Janus)	**1974**	(1)
	Misty (Janus)	**1975**	(2)
Billy Swan	*I Can Help* (Monument)	**1974**	(6)
Mitchell Torok	*When Mexico Gave Up The Rumba* (Brunswick)	**1956**	(6)
Conway Twitty	*It's Only Make Believe* (MGM)	**1958**	(1)
	Mona Lisa (MGM)	**1959**	(5)
Leroy Van Dyke	*Walk On By* (Mercury)	**1962**	(5)
Slim Whitman	*Rose Marie* (London)	**1955**	(1)
	Indian Love Call (London)	**1955**	(7)
	China Doll (London)	**1955**	(15)
	Tumbling Tumbleweeds (London)	**1956**	(19)
	I'm A Fool (London)	**1956**	(16)
	Serenade (London)	**1956**	(8)
	I'll Take You Home Again Kathleen (London	**1957**	(7)
	Happy Anniversary (United Artists)	**1974**	(14)
Don Williams	*I Recall A Gypsy Woman* (ABC)	**1976**	(13)
Sheb Wooley	*Purple People Eater* (MGM)	**1958**	(12)
Tammy Wynette	*Stand By Your Man* (Epic)	**1975**	(1)
	D.I.V.O.R.C.E. (Epic)	**1975**	(12)
Faron Young	*It's Four In The Morning* (Mercury)	**1972**	(3)

Slim Whitman

Billie Jo Spears

Jim Reeves

Hank Locklin

. . . and British Country favorites

At the end of 1979, the leading British publication *Country Music People* asked its readers to choose the "Artist Of The Decade." It is interesting to note that several very popular American stars are low down on the list while some less-known acts are highly rated; that artists who have made several visits to the UK have done well, like Don Williams, Billie Jo Spears and Johnny Cash; and that British fans are very loyal, sticking with their favorites for many years – like Slim Whitman, Jean Shepard and, incredibly for a poll about important artists of the seventies, Jim Reeves, who died in 1964.

1	Don Williams	29	Jim Reeves
2	Slim Whitman	30	Glaser Brothers
3	Dolly Parton	31	Conway Twitty
4	Johnny Cash	32	Sammi Smith
5	Merle Haggard	33	Donna Fargo
6	Billie Jo Spears	34	Barbara Fairchild
7	Boxcar Willie	35	Porter Wagoner
8	Marty Robbins	36	Elvis Presley
9	Emmylou Harris	37	Kris Kristofferson
10	Tammy Wynette	38	The Hillsiders
11	Waylon Jennings	39	Ronnie Milsap
12	George Jones	40	John Denver
13	Crystal Gayle	41	Mickey Newbury
14	George Hamilton IV	42	Pete Sayers
15	Charley Pride	43	Dave and Sugar
16	Kenny Rogers	44	Roger Miller
17	Willie Nelson	45	Gary Stewart
18	Jean Shepard	46	Hank Locklin
19	Statler Brothers	47	Hank Snow
20	Bobby Bare	48	Vernon Oxford
21	Loretta Lynn	49	Ray Price
22	Faron Young	50	Chet Atkins
23	Larry Gatlin		
24	Tom T. Hall		
25	Gene Watson		
26	Moe Bandy		
27	Oak Ridge Boys		
28	Bill Anderson		

EVERYTHING I'VE ALWAYS WANTED

Porter Wagoner's list of his most important achievements

Porter Wagoner is one of Country music's most colorful characters and longest-running success stories. Internationally known for his flashy Nudie suits, he's also been an important innovator in Nashville; one of the first artists to produce his own records, the first Country entertainer to host his own syndicated TV show, and the first to suggest an annual celebration for Country music fans – an idea which evolved into the highly successful Fan Fair, held each June in Nashville. He's keenly aware of the link between soul and Country and has brought black entertainers to perform and record in Nashville, saying, "There is such a similarity between black music and Country music – the feeling, the sincerity." Porter worked with Dolly Parton for several years on his TV shows and they recorded numerous successful duets. Off duty, Porter is an avid fisherman.

1. Discovering Dolly Parton
2. Inviting James Brown to appear at the Grand Ole Opry
3. Hosting the longest-running American Country music television show. It ran for twenty years
4. Producing a rhythm and blues album on Joe Simon
5. Catching a ten-pound large-mouth bass at Center Hill Lake

Left: Porter Wagoner today

Right: Porter Wagoner with Dolly Parton

FIND OUT WHAT'S HAPPENING

The fan club list . . .

This fan club list could have been much longer – and much less useful. There are hundreds of fan clubs in Country music and they vary enormously in reliability and what they offer to members. For this reason we've decided to limit the list to the clubs we consider fairly stable and those devoted to well-known stars. Several are excellent and have been established for years, notably the Loretta Lynn Fan Club which has been going for over two decades. Loudilla, Loretta and Kay Johnson, who have always run Loretta Lynn's club, are also responsible for the International Fan Club Organization, which monitors and assists registered clubs, and we're grateful for their recommendations, which are included in this list.

If you are writing for details to any of these clubs please enclose a stamped addressed envelope or (if writing from abroad) an International Reply Coupon.

Free Alabama Fan Club
Casey Case, PO Box 529, Fort Payne, Alabama 35967, USA

Bill Anderson Fan Club
Jeanne Gaddis, PO Box 514, Madison, Tennessee 37115, USA

John Anderson International Fan Club
Deeanna Anderson Wall, PO Box 1679, Hendersonville, Tennessee 37075, USA

Moe Bandy Fan Club
Encore Talent, 2137 Zercher Road, San Antonio, Texas 78209, USA

Bobby Bare Fan Club
Greil Works Management, Box 120681, Nashville, Tennessee 37272, USA

Bellamy Brothers Fan Club
Barbara La Frandre, PO Box 3153, Winter Haven, Florida 33880, USA

Boxcar Willie Fan Club
Jean Bryant, Rt 1, Box 93, Lexington, Georgia 30648, USA

Ed Bruce Fan Club
Martha Dozier, 1022 16th Avenue South, Nashville, Tennessee 37212, USA

Glen Campbell Fan Club
Box 69500, Hollywood, California 90069, USA

Johnny and June Carter Cash Fan Club
Charles & Virginia Stohler, 1110 W Hartman Road, Anderson, Indiana 46011, USA

European Johnny Cash Fan Club
Elvira & Jan Flederus, Postbus 17, 7720 AA Dalfsen, Holland

Roy Clark Fan Club
3225 South Norwood, Tulsa, Oklahoma 74135, USA

World Family Of John Denver
Joanne Chapelo, PO Box 5973, Cleveland, Ohio 44101, USA

Janie Fricke Fan Club
Floreine Jackson, 301 La Casa Drive, 504, Kerrville, Texas 78028, USA

David Frizzell and Shelly West Fan Club
Opal Stevens, Box 267, Lakeview, Ohio 43331, USA

Crystal Gayle Fan Club
Gayle Enterprises, 51 Music Square East, Nashville, Tennessee 37203, USA

Mickey Gilley Fan Club
Sherwood Cryer, 4500 Spencer Highway, Pasadena, Texas 77504, USA

Lee Greenwood Fan Club
Debbie Durham, 2 Music Circle South, Nashville, Tennessee 37203, USA

Emmylou Harris Fan Club
Box 248, Rodeo, California 94512, USA

George Jones Fan Club Inc
Gerald Murray, 2903 Woodward Avenue, Muscle Shoals, Alabama 35660, USA

Kris Kristofferson International Fan Club
Jerri Smith, 200 Drescent Drive, Littlefield, Texas 79339, USA

Brenda Lee Fan Club
John W. Smith III, 2126 N. North Street, Peoria, Illinois 61604, USA

Johnny Lee Fan Club
Sherwood Cryer, 4500 Spencer Highway, Pasadena, Texas 77504, USA

Jerry Lee Lewis International Fan Club
Barrie Gamblin, 16 Milton Road, Wimbledon, London SW19, England

Loretta Lynn Fan Club
Loudilla, Loretta and Kay Johnson, Box 177, Wild Horse, Colorado 80862, USA

Barbara Mandrell

Barbara Mandrell Fan Club
Bettye Anderson, PO Box 620, Hendersonville, Tennessee 37075, USA

Reba McEntire Fan Club
George A. Wooding, Jr, Rt 1, Box 223, Bon Aqua, Tennessee 37025, USA

Bill Monroe Fan Club
Lynda Bowman, Rt 2, Box 195–F, Meadows Of Dan, Virginia 24120, USA

Willie Nelson Fan Club
Jan Coney, PO Box 571, Danbury, Connecticut 06810, USA

The Oak Ridge Boys Fan Club
Kathy McClintock, 329 Rockland Road, Hendersonville, Tennessee 37075, USA

Gram Parsons Memorial Foundation
Mark Holland, 3109 Ola Avenue, Tampa, Florida 33603, USA

Dolly Parton Fan Club
Box 4499, North Hollywood, California 91607, USA

Ray Price Fan Club
Mike Grulkey, Rt 3, Box 144, Huntsville, Arizona 72740, USA

Ronnie Prophet Fan Club
Ann Kowal, 1392 Queen Street East, Toronto, Ontario, Canada

Eddie Rabbitt Fan Club
Sandy Burnside, PO Box 125, Lewistown, Ohio 43333, USA

Jerry Reed Fan Club
Janet Buffalow, 13814 South 8th Street, Grandview, Missouri 64030, USA

Jim Reeves Fan Club
Jim Reeves Enterprises, Drawer 1, Madison, Tennessee 37115, USA

Kenny Rogers' Special Friends
8265 Beverly Boulevard, Los Angeles, California 90048, USA

T.G. Sheppard Fan Club
Nancy Van Putte, 70 English Road, Rochester, New York 14616, USA

Ricky Skaggs Fan Club
PO Box 171080, Nashville, Tennessee 37217, USA

Sylvia Fan Club
Mike Allen, PO Box 150912, Nashville, Tennessee 37215, USA

B.J. Thomas Fan Club
PO Box 120003, Arlington, Texas 76012, USA

Ernest Tubb Fan Club
Norma Barthel, Rt 1, Box 126, Roland, Oklahoma 74954, USA

Conway Twitty Fan Club
Twitty City, 1 Music Village Boulevard, Hendersonville, Tennessee 37075, USA

Porter Wagoner Fan Club
Debra Loy, PO Box 557, Columbia, Kentucky 42728, USA

Slim Whitman Appreciation Society of the United States
Loren R. Knapp, 1002 West Thurber Street, Tucson, Arizona 85705, USA

Hank Williams Jr Fan Club
Diana Caldwell, Box 1061, Cullman, Alabama 35055, USA

Tammy Wynette Fan Club
Jackie Paule, 6 Music Circle North, Nashville, Tennessee 37203, USA

Faron Young Fan Club
Yvonne Garner, PO Box 1782, Pasadena, Texas 77501, USA

. . . with Country star addresses

So you want to write to your favorite Country star? You know that entertainers are busy people and you may not get a personal reply, but you'll be happy if there's a good chance the letter will be read by the star in question. Writing c/o record companies is an uncertain business; they are busy too, frequently dealing with dozens of different acts, and although they try to help, fan letters often go astray. By far the best method is to write c/o the artist's personal manager, who's unlikely to have more than a handful of clients and is invariably in daily contact with each one.

Alabama	c/o Dale Morris & Associates, 812 19th Avenue South, Nashville, Tennessee 37203, USA
Bobby Bare	c/o Greilworks, PO Box 120681, Nashville, Tennessee 37212, USA
Ed Bruce	c/o Patsy Bruce, PO Box 120428, Nashville, Tennessee 37212, USA
Johnny Cash	c/o Reba Hancock, House Of Cash, PO Box 508, Hendersonville, Tennessee 37075, USA
John Conlee	c/o Dick Kent, PO Box 53, Nashville, Tennessee 37221, USA

John Co

Mac Davis   Waylon Jennings

Mac Davis	c/o Sandy Gallin, Katz-Gallin-Morey, 9255 Sunset Boulevard, Suite 1115, Los Angeles, California 90069, USA
Janie Fricke	c/o Randy Jackson, Chardon Inc, 3198 Royal Lane, Suite 204, Dallas, Texas 75229, USA
Crystal Gayle	c/o Bill Gatzimos, Crystal Gayle Enterprises, 51 Music Square East, Nashville, Tennessee 37203, USA
Merle Haggard	c/o Tex Whitson, PO Box 500, Bella Vista, California 96008, USA
Emmylou Harris	c/o Eddie Tickner, Box 4471, North Hollywood, California 91607, USA
Waylon Jennings	c/o Management III, 9744 Wilshire Boulevard, Beverly Hills, California 90212, USA
Barbara Mandrell	c/o Irby Mandrell, 38 Music Square East, Nashville, Tennessee 37203, USA

Ronnie Milsap

Ronnie Milsap	c/o Dan Cleary, BNB Management, 9454 Wilshire Boulevard, No 309, Beverly Hills, California 90212, USA
Willie Nelson	c/o Mark Rothbaum, 225 Main Street, Danbury, Connecticut 06810, USA
Dolly Parton	c/o Sandy Gallin, Katz-Gallin-Morey, 9255 Sunset Boulevard, Suite 1115, Los Angeles, California 90069, USA
Charley Pride	c/o Cecca Productions, PO Box 30507, Dallas, Texas 75230, USA
Jerry Reed	c/o Frank Rodgers, Vector Music, 1107 18th Avenue South, Nashville, Tennessee 37212, USA
T.G. Sheppard	c/o Jack D. Johnson Talent, PO Box 40484, Nashville, Tennessee 37204, USA
Ricky Skaggs	c/o Chip Peay, PO Box 15871, Nashville, Tennessee 37215, USA
Sylvia	c/o Randy Jackson, Chardon Inc, 3198 Royal Lane, Suite 204, Dallas, Texas 75229, USA
Hank Williams, Jr	c/o James R. Smith, PO Box 790, Cullman, Alabama 35055, USA
Tammy Wynette	c/o George Richey, Tammy Wynette Enterprises, 6 Music Circle North, Nashville, Tennessee 37203, USA

Having noted the stars' fan clubs and addresses, here are some colorful poses of the stars themselves appearing in alphabetical order...

Above: Alabama   *Below*: Moe Bandy

Left: Bobby Bare   *Above*: Johnny Cash   *Below*: Roy Clark

Above: Freddy Fender   *Right*: Janie Fricke

Left: Crystal Gayle   *Above*: Merle Haggard   *Below*: Emmylou Harris

Left: Johnny Lee   *Above*: Reba McEntire

Left: Oak Ridge Boys   *Above*: Kenny Rogers and Dolly Parton

Above: Ray Price   *Below*: Ricky Skaggs   *Right*: Conway Twitty

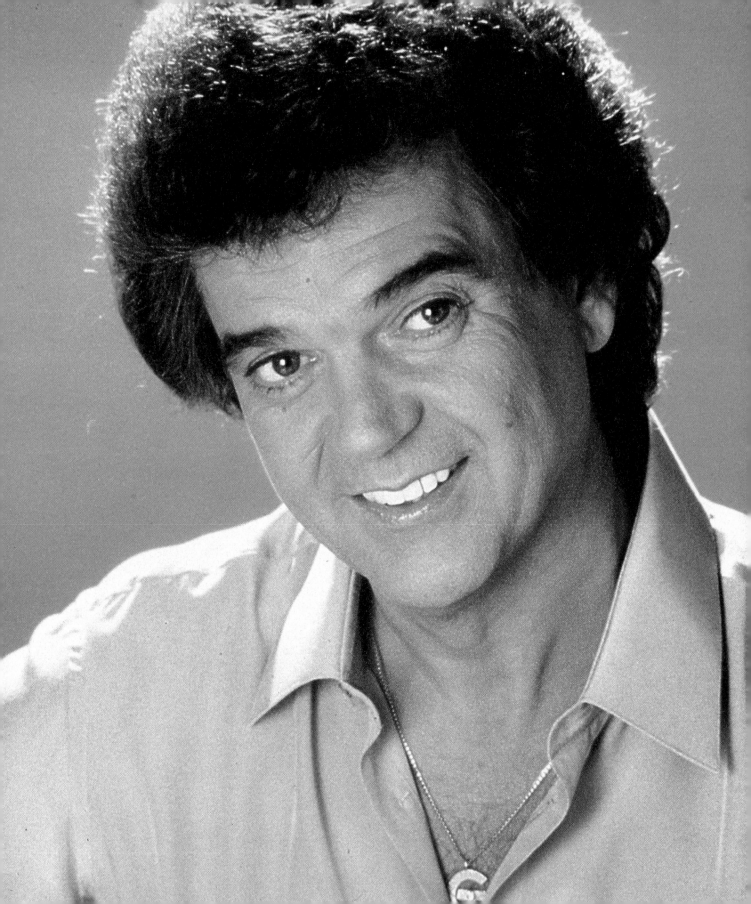

Left: Don Williams *Above*: Hank Williams, Jr

Above: Tammy Wynette

FOR THE GOOD TIMES

Ray Price lists his non-musical activities

Horses

I raise thoroughbred horses. Some of my brood stock came from England, from a line of Derby winners. I had one of the last sons of Hyperion and I also had a son of Tudor Minstrel. Nowadays I don't go in for it in such a big way, I can't get the help that I need. So I just have a handful of horses around now.

Dogs

I raise greyhounds. Not that many, it's not a big operation but I enjoy doing it.

Pigeons

I have a lot of English homing pigeons though I don't get a chance to race them like I once did. A friend of mine called Masserella lives in Leicester, in England, and he raises top champion English pigeons. He also makes ice cream in that area.

Fox-hunting

My dad was a great fox-hunter. He was of Welsh descent. I believe we were Welsh about the time of my great-great grandfather. It's said that the Price castle still stands in Wales but I can't believe that Price was any kind of royal name. I guess it'd be more associated with horse-thieves or something!

Quail-shooting

I hunted in the Grand National quail hunt in Oklahoma during 1977 – and I won! Mind you, I was a new shooter in that competition and I wasn't handicapped like some of the others. But the killing is not where it's at. It's the way the dogs are handled and other outside things. I don't love to hunt as much as I once did. But you see, when I was a boy, I was raised on a farm and we had to hunt just to get meat on the table – things were that bad during the depression.

FORT WORTH, DALLAS OR HOUSTON

Musicians and singers who were Texas born

Duane Allen	Taylorville, April 29, 1943
Gene Autry	Tioga, September 29, 1907
Johnny Bond	Houston, February 17, 1935
Don Bowman	Lubbock, August 26, 1937
Boxcar Willie	Sterret, September 1, 1931
Bill Boyd	Fannin County, September 29, 1910
Milton Brown	Stephenville, September 8, 1903
Guy Clark	Rockport, November 6, 1941
Vernon Dalhart	Jefferson, April 6, 1883
Mac Davis	Lubbock, January 21, 1942
Eddie Dean	Posey, July 9, 1907
Jimmy Dean	Plainview, August 10, 1928
Al Dexter	Jacksonville, May 4, 1905
Dottsy	Sequin, April 6, 1953
Johnny Duncan	Dublin, October 5, 1938
Tommy Duncan	Hillsboro, January 11, 1911

Guy Clark

Joe Ely	Amarillo, February 9, 1947
Dale Evans	Ulvalda, October 31, 1912
Freddy Fender	San Benito, June 4, 1937
Kinky Friedman	Rio Duckworth, October 31, 1944
Lefty Frizzell	Corsicana, March 31, 1928
Steve Fromholz	Temple, June 8, 1945
Larry Gatlin	Odessa, May 2, 1948
Johnny Gimble	Tyler, May 30, 1926
Claude Gray	Henderson, January 25, 1932
Monte Hale	San Angelo, June 8, 1921
Stuart Hamblen	Kellyville, October 20, 1908
Don Henley	Gilmer, July 22, 1947
Goldie Hill	Karnes County, January 11, 1933
Buddy Holly	Lubbock, September 7, 1936
Johnny Horton	Tyler, April 3, 1929
Waylon Jennings	Littlefield, June 15, 1937
George Jones	Saratoga, September 12, 1931
Kris Kristofferson	Brownsville, June 22, 1937
Dolly Laverne	Muleshoe, December 11, 1915
Millie Laverne	Muleshoe, April 11, 1913
Johnny Lee	Texas City, July 3, 1946
Bob Luman	Nacogdoches, April 15, 1937
Leon McAuliffe	Houston, January 3, 1917
Red River Dave McEnery	San Antonio, December 15, 1914
Barbara Mandrell	Houston, December 25, 1948
Louise Mandrell	Corpus Christi, July 13, 1954
Roger Miller	Fort Worth, January 2, 1936
Moon Mullican	Corrigan, March 29, 1909
Jerry Naylor	Stephenville, March 6, 1939

Willie Nelson	Abbott, April 30, 1933
Mike Nesmith	Houston, December 30, 1942
Eddie Noack	Houston, April 29, 1930
Roy Orbison	Vernon, April 23, 1936
Buck Owens	Sherman, August 12, 1929
Leon Payne	Alba, June 15, 1917
Ray Price	Perryville, January 12, 1926
Goebel Reeves	Sherman, October 9, 1899
Jim Reeves	Galloway, Panola County, August 20, 1923
Jeannie C. Riley	Anson, October 19, 1945
Tex Ritter	Murvaul, Panola County, January 12, 1905
Johnny Rodriguez	Sabinal, December 10, 1951
Kenny Rogers	Houston, August 21, 1938
Doug Sahm	San Antonio, November 6, 1942
Billy Joe Shaver	Corsicana, 1941
Billie Jo Spears	Beaumont, January 14, 1937
Nat Stuckey	Cass County, December 17, 1937
Hank Thompson	Waco, September 3, 1925
Ernest Tubb	Crisp, February 9, 1914
Justin Tubb	San Antonio, August 30, 1935
Tanya Tucker	Seminole, October 10, 1958
Charlie Waller	Jointerville, January 19, 1935
Jacky Ward	Groveton, November 18, 1946
Gene Watson	Palestine, October 11, 1943
Don Williams	Floydada, June 18, 1947
Foy Willing	Bosque County, 1915
Bob Wills	Koss, Limestone County, March 6, 1905

Billy Joe Shaver

Hank Thompson and the Brazos Valley Boys

A FOUR-LEGGED FRIEND

Talented horses of singing cowboys

Koko

"The Miracle Horse of the Movies" belonged to Rex Allen, who made 19 movies for Republic between 1950 and 1954. Koko originally belonged to Dale Evans but proved too wild. Trained by Glen Randall, the trainer of Trigger, Roy Rogers' horse, he became pretty adept at all the roll-over-and-play-dead tricks required for silver screen fame. The only problem was his markings, which meant that a double couldn't be found and all close-up work had to be done by Koko himself. Koko toured the rodeo circuit with Allen for many years but finally went to the great rodeo in the sky during 1971.

Trigger

The smartest horse in Hollywood cost just $2,500. Glen Randall began training him for Roy Rogers in 1941, teaching him tricks, including the ability to untie another horse, take a pistol out of its holster and walk for a considerable distance on hind legs only. There were at least two other Triggers – Little Trigger, who did all the personal appearances, and Trigger Jr, who was understudy to both horses. The original Trigger retired in 1957 at the age of 25 and lived to be 33. After the horse's death, Roy Rogers had Trigger's remains mounted and placed on display in the Roy Rogers–Dale Evans Museum at Victoriaville, California.

Buttermilk

Dale Evans' horse, a gentle animal that appeared in countless movies. When Buttermilk died, it too was mounted and placed in the Rogers–Evans Museum, alongside Trigger, and Autry's dog Bullet.

Champion

Gene Autry's horse and the only one of his breed to eventually star in his own TV show. Actually, three different Champions starred on film throughout the years and each of these had several understudies – all chestnuts with a blaze face and four white-stockinged feet. In his autobiography, Autry commented that the original Champion possessed no less than four stand-ins while Greta Garbo, perhaps the foremost star of her day, possessed but one! It was this animal that died from a heart attack in 1944, while Autry was involved on war duties, and was later buried at the star's famous Melody Ranch.

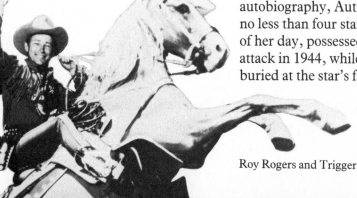

Roy Rogers and Trigger

GETTING BY HIGH AND STRANGE

Kris Kristofferson's occupations before he became a star

Few Country entertainers can have had such a wide range of occupations as Kris Kristofferson. He always wanted to write and as a student took all kinds of Jack London-type manual jobs in his vacations for the sake of experience. Since finding fame as a songwriter and singer, Kris has become a very successful film actor.

Footballer	Kris played American football, for the Pomona College, California team, while he was a student.
Boxer	He was a gifted boxer in his teens and fought in the Golden Gloves championship. He bears a boxer's droop over his left eye as a permanent reminder of those days.
Writer	While at Pomona College Kris won the top four out of 20 prizes in the *Atlantic Monthly* collegiate short story contest. He subsequently wrote a novel, though it was never published.
Student	Kris won a Rhodes Scholarship to Oxford University, England, where he studied English Literature.
Singer and Songwriter	Kris found time to sing and write songs while in England. He adopted the name "Kris Carson" but was unsuccessful in attracting the attention of anyone who could have furthered his career as a performer.
Soldier	He spent four years in the US Army, went through jump school and flight training, and left with the rank of Captain. He was on his way to West Point to teach English Literature when he made the sudden decision to go to Nashville.
Janitor	He took over Billy Swan's job as janitor of the CBS studio in Nashville in the mid-sixties. "Bob Dylan was the first person I emptied ashtrays for."
Bartender	At the famous Tally Ho Tavern in Nashville, Tennessee.
Helicopter Pilot	To off-shore oil rigs in the Gulf of Mexico.

Kris Kristoffe

GOLDEN TEARS

The bestselling albums in Country history

Gold records were first certified by the RIAA (Recording Industry Association of America) in 1958. A Gold album is awarded for sales of 500,000 and a Platinum album(★) is awarded for sales of 1,000,000.

1959 Tennessee Ernie Ford *Hymns* (Capitol)

1961 Tennessee Ernie Ford *Spirituals* (Capitol)
Jimmy Dean *Big Bad John* (Columbia)

1962 Tennessee Ernie Ford *Star Carol* (Capitol)
Tennessee Ernie Ford *Nearer The Cross* (Capitol)

1964 Johnny Horton *Johnny Horton's Greatest Hits* (Columbia)

1965 Johnny Cash *Ring Of Fire* (Columbia)
Roger Miller *Return Of Roger Miller* (Smash)
Marty Robbins *Gunfighter Ballads And Trail Songs* (Columbia)

1966 Roger Miller *Golden Hits* (Smash)
Eddy Arnold *My World* (RCA)
Jim Reeves *The Best Of Jim Reeves* (RCA)
Roger Miller *Dang Me* (Smash)

1967 Johnny Cash *I Walk The Line* (Columbia)
Bobbie Gentry *Ode To Billie Joe* (Capitol)

1968
Jim Reeves *Distant Drums* (RCA)
Buck Owens *Best Of Buck Owens* (Capitol)
Eddy Arnold *Best of Eddy Arnold* (RCA)
Glen Campbell *By The Time I Get To Phoenix* (Capitol)
Glen Campbell *Gentle On My Mind* (Capitol)
Johnny Cash *Johnny Cash At Folsom Prison* (Capitol)
Jeannie C. Riley *Harper Valley PTA* (Plantation)

1969
Glen Campbell *Hey Little One* (Capitol)
Glen Campbell and Bobbie Gentry *Gentry/Campbell* (Capitol)
Glen Campbell *Galveston* (Capitol)
Hank Williams *Hank Williams' Greatest Hits* (MGM)
Hank Williams *Your Cheatin' Heart* (MGM)
Ray Stevens *Gitarzan* (Monument)
Johnny Cash *Johnny Cash's Greatest Hits* (Columbia)
Johnny Cash *Johnny Cash At San Quentin* (Columbia)
Glen Campbell *Glenn Campbell Live* (Capitol)
Gene Autry *Rudolph The Red-Nosed Reindeer* (Columbia)

1970
Charley Pride *The Best Of Charley Pride* (RCA)
Johnny Cash *Hello, I'm Johnny Cash* (Columbia)
Glen Campbell *Try A Little Kindness* (Capitol)
Loretta Lynn *Don't Come Home A-Drinkin'* (Decca)
Tammy Wynette *Tammy's Greatest Hits* (Epic)

1971
Charley Pride *Charley Pride's 10th Album* (RCA)
Charley Pride *Just Plain Charley* (RCA)
Charley Pride *Charley Pride In Person* (RCA)
Ray Price *For The Good Times* (Columbia)
Merle Haggard *The Fightin' Side Of Me* (Capitol)
Lynn Anderson *Rose Garden* (Columbia)
Johnny Cash *The World Of Johnny Cash* (Columbia)

1972
Loretta Lynn *Loretta Lynn's Greatest Hits* (Decca)
Charley Pride *Charley Pride Sings Heart Songs* (RCA)
Glen Campbell *Glen Campbell's Greatest Hits* (Capitol)
Conway Twitty *Hello Darlin'* (Decca)
Freddie Hart *Easy Lovin'* (Capitol)
Merle Haggard *The Best Of Merle Haggard* (Capitol)

1973
Donna Fargo *The Happiest Girl In The Whole USA* (Dot)
Kenny Rogers and The First Edition *Kenny Rogers and The First Edition Greatest Hits* (Warner/Reprise)
Charley Pride *The Sensational Charley Pride* (RCA)
Charley Pride *From Me To You* (RCA)
Charley Pride *The Country Way* (RCA)
Kris Kristofferson *The Silver-Tongued Devil And I* (Monument)
Charlie Rich *Behind Closed Doors* (Epic)
Kris Kristofferson *Jesus Was A Capricorn* (Monument)
Anne Murray *Snowbird* (Capitol)

1974   Charlie Rich *Very Special Love Song* (Epic)
Mac Davis *Stop And Smell The Roses* (Columbia)
Charlie Rich *There Won't Be Anymore* (RCA)
Kris Kristofferson *Me And Bobby McGee* (Monument)

1975   Charley Pride *Did You Think To Pray* (RCA)
Charley Pride *(Country) Charley Pride* (RCA)
Charlie Daniels Band *Fire On The Mountain* (Kama Sutra)
Freddy Fender *Before The Next Teardrop Falls* (ABC/Dot)
Glen Campbell *Rhinestone Cowboy* (Capitol)

1976   C.W. McCall *Black Bear Road* (MGM)
Willie Nelson *Red-Headed Stranger* (Columbia)
Waylon Jennings, Willie Nelson, Tompall Glaser and Jessi Colter *The Outlaws* (RCA)★
Mac Davis *All The Love In The World* (Columbia)
Glen Campbell *The Christmas Feeling* (Capitol)

1977   Hank Williams *24 Greatest Hits* (Polydor/MGM)
The Statler Brothers *The Best Of The Statler Brothers* (Phonogram/Mercury)
Waylon Jennings *Dreaming My Dreams* (RCA)
Waylon Jennings *Ol' Waylon* (RCA)★
Waylon Jennings *Are You Ready For The Country?* (RCA)
Kenny Rogers *Kenny Rogers* (United Artists)
Glen Campbell *Southern Nights* (Capitol)
Johnny Cash *The Johnny Cash Portrait/His Greatest Hits Vol. III* (Columbia)
Crystal Gayle *We Must Believe In Magic* (United Artists)★
Kenny Rogers *Daytime Friends* (United Artists)
Dolly Parton *Here You Come Again* (RCA)★

1978   Waylon Jennings *Waylon Live* (RCA)
Waylon Jennings and Willie Nelson *Waylon And Willie* (RCA)★
Ronnie Milsap *It Was Almost Like A Song* (RCA)
Kenny Rogers *Ten Years Of Gold* (RCA)★
Willie Nelson *The Sound In Your Mind* (Columbia)
Dolly Parton *The Best Of Dolly Parton* (RCA)
Willie Nelson *Stardust* (Columbia)
Emmylou Harris *Elite Hotel* (Warner Bros)
Crystal Gayle *When I Dream* (United Artists)
Waylon Jennings *I've Always Been Crazy* (RCA)
Ronnie Milsap *Only One Love In My Life* (RCA)
Anne Murray *Let's Keep It That Way* (Capitol)
Dolly Parton *Heartbreaker* (RCA)
Kenny Rogers *Love Or Something Like It* (United Artists)
Kenny Rogers *The Gambler* (United Artists)★

1979 Charlie Daniels Band *Million Mile Reflections* (Epic)★
Anne Murray *New Kind Of Feeling* (Capitol)
Waylon Jennings *Greatest Hits* (RCA)★
Ronnie Milsap *Ronnie Milsap Live* (RCA)
Willie Nelson *Willie Nelson And Family Live* (Columbia)
Willie Nelson and Leon Russell *One For The Road* (Columbia)
Dolly Parton *Great Balls Of Fire* (RCA)
Tanya Tucker *TNT* (MCA)
Kenny Rogers and Dottie West *Classics* (United Artists)

1980 Crystal Gayle *Miss The Mississippi* (Columbia)
Kenny Rogers *Kenny* (United Artists)★
Annie Murray *I'll Always Love You* (Capitol)
Waylon Jennings *What Goes Around* (RCA)
Crystal Gayle *Classic Crystal* (United Artists)
Oak Ridge Boys *Y'all Come Back Saloon* (MCA)
Kenny Rogers *Gideon* (United Artists)★
Larry Gatlin *Straight Ahead* (Columbia)
Various Artists *Urban Cowboy/Original Soundtrack* (Asylum)
Waylon Jennings *Music Man* (RCA)
Oak Ridge Boys *The Oak Ridge Boys Have Arrived* (MCA)
Don Williams *The Best Of Don Williams, Vol. II* (MCA)
Oak Ridge Boys *Together* (MCA)
Eddie Rabbitt *Horizon* (Elektra)
Eddie Rabbitt *The Best Of Eddie Rabbitt* (Elektra)
Anne Murray *Greatest Hits* (Capitol)★
Kenny Rogers *Greatest Hits* (United Artists)★
Don Williams *I Believe In You* (MCA)
Charlie Daniels Band *Full Moon* (Epic)★
Willie Nelson *Willie Nelson Sings Kris Kristofferson* (Columbia)
Willie Nelson *Honeysuckle Rose/Original Soundtrack* (Columbia)

1981 Barbara Mandrell *Best Of Barbara Mandrell* (MCA)
Oak Ridge Boys *Greatest Hits* (MCA)★
Emmylou Harris *Luxury Liner* (Warner Bros)

Ronnie Milsap *Greatest Hits* (RCA)★
Emmylou Harris *Blue Kentucky Girl* (Warner Bros)
Emmylou Harris *Profile – Best Of Emmylou Harris* (Warner Bros)
Statler Brothers *Best Of The Statlers* (Mercury/Phonogram)
Eddie Rabbitt *Horizon* (Elektra)★
Mac Davis *It's Hard To Be Humble* (Mercury/Phonogram)
Dolly Parton *9 To 5 And Odd Jobs* (RCA)
Emmylou Harris *Roses In The Snow* (Warner Bros)
Willie Nelson *Somewhere Over The Rainbow* (Columbia)★
Alabama *Feels So Right* (RCA)★
Statler Brothers *The Originals* (Mercury/Phonogram)
Anne Murray *Where Do You Go When You Dream* (Capitol)
Alabama *My Home's In Alabama* (RCA)★
Oak Ridge Boys *Fancy Free* (MCA)★
Kenny Rogers *Share Your Love* (Liberty)★
The Charlie Daniels Band *Saddle Tramp* (Liberty)
Larry Gatlin and The Gatlin Brothers Band *Greatest Hits* (Columbia)
Waylon Jennings and Jessi Colter *Leather And Lace* (RCA)
George Jones *I Am What I Am* (Epic)
Emmylou Harris *Evangeline* (Warner Bros)
Loretta Lynn *Greatest Hits – Volume II* (MCA)
Eddie Rabbitt *Step By Step* (Elektra)
Conway Twitty *Greatest Hits – Volume II* (Decca)
Conway Twitty and Loretta Lynn *Lead Me On* (Decca)
Hank Williams Jr *Whiskey Bent And Hell Bound* (Warner/Curb)
Willie Nelson *Greatest Hits (And Some That Will Be)* (Columbia)★
Ronnie Milsap *There's No Gettin' Over Me* (RCA)
Various Artists *Coal Miner's Daughter – Original Soundtrack* (MCA)

1982   Kenny Rogers *Christmas* (Liberty)★
Barbara Mandrell *Live* (MCA)
Oak Ridge Boys *Bobby Sue* (MCA)
Hank Williams Jr *The Pressure Is On* (Elektra)
Alabama *Mountain Music* (RCA)★
Juice Newton *Juice* (Capitol)★
Willie Nelson *Always On My Mind* (Columbia)★
Johnny Lee *Lookin' For Love* (Asylum)
Crystal Gayle *When I Dream* (Liberty)★
Juice Newton *Quiet Lies* (Capitol)
Kenny Rogers *Love Will Turn You Around* (Liberty)
Statler Brothers *Christmas Card* (Polygram)
Anne Murray *Christmas Wishes* (Capitol)
Charlie Daniels Band *Windows* (Epic)
Willie Nelson *Pretty Paper* (Columbia)
Oak Ridge Boys *Christmas* (MCA)
Ray Price *All Time Greatest Hits* (Columbia)
Marty Robbins *All Time Greatest Hits* (Columbia)

HANK WILLIAMS YOU WROTE MY LIFE

A selected list of biographies and autobiographies

Tammy Wynette
: *Stand By Your Man* Tammy Wynette with Joan Dew (Simon & Schuster USA; Arrow Books UK)

Bob Wills
: *San Antonio Rose* Charles Townsend (University of Illinois Press USA)

Merle Haggard
: *Sing Me Back Home* Merle Haggard with Peggy Russell (Times Books USA)

Tex Ritter
: *The Tex Ritter Story* Johnny Bond (Chappell USA)

Jeannie C. Riley
: *From Harper Valley To The Mountain Top* Jeannie C. Riley (Chosen USA)

Hank Williams
: *Your Cheatin' Heart* Chet Flippo (Simon & Schuster USA; Eel Pie UK)

Johnny Cash
: *The Man In Black* Johnny Cash (Zondervan USA)
Winners Got Scars Too Christopher S. Wren (Dial USA; Abacus UK)

Dolly Parton
: *Dolly* Alanna Nash (Reed USA)
Daughter Of The South Lola Scobey (Kensington USA)

77

Roy Acuff	*Smokey Mountain Boy* Elizabeth Schlappi (Pelican USA)
Jimmie Rodgers	*Jimmie Rodgers* Nolan Porterfield (Urbana USA)
Loretta Lynn	*Coal Miner's Daughter* Loretta Lynn with George Vecsey (Warner Books USA)
Waylon Jennings and Willie Nelson	*Waylon Jennings and Willie Nelson* Bob Allen (Quick Fox USA)
Patsy Cline	*Patsy Cline* Ellis Nassour (Tower USA)
Glen Campbell	*The Glen Campbell Story* Freda Kramer (Pyramid USA)
Willie Nelson	*Willie Nelson – Country Outlaw* Lola Scobey (Zebra USA) *Willie Nelson Family Album* Lana Nelson Fowler (H.M. Poirot USA)
Minnie Pearl	*An Autobiography* Minnie Pearl (Pocket Books USA)
Mandrell Sisters	*The Mandrell Family Album* Louise Mandrell and Ace Collins (Thomas Nelson USA)
Elvis Presley	*Elvis* Jerry Hopkins (Simon & Schuster USA; Abacus UK) *Elvis – The Final Years* Jerry Hopkins (St Martins USA; W.H. Allen UK)
Alton Delmore	*Truth Is Stranger Than Publicity* Alton Delmore with Charles K. Wolfe (Country Music Foundation USA)
Hank Williams Jr	*Living Proof* Hank Williams Jr (Dell/Putnam USA)
B.J. Thomas	*Home Is Where I Belong* B.J. Thomas with Jerry B. Jenkins (Word USA)
Jerry Lee Lewis	*Great Balls Of Fire* Myra Lewis with Murray Silver (Quill Books USA; Virgin UK)
Tom T. Hall	*The Storyteller's Nashville* Tom T. Hall (Doubleday USA)
Buddy Holly	*Buddy Holly – His Life And Music* John J. Goldrosen (Quick Fox USA; Panther UK)
David Allan Coe	*Just For The Record* David Allan Coe (self-published)
Gene Autry	*Back In The Saddle Again* Gene Autry with Mickey Herskowitz (Doubleday USA)

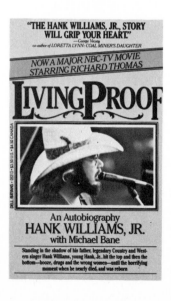

HOLD WHAT YOU'VE GOT

Sonny James' incredible run of consecutive Number One hits

Sixteen Number Ones in the Billboard chart – all in a row. Not bad going for a singer whose first Number One was "Young Love" – in 1956!

1967   *Need You*
I'll Never Find Another You
It's The Little Things

1968   *A World Of Our Own*
Heaven Says Hello
Born To Be With You

1969   *Only The Lonely*
Running Bear
Since I Met You Baby

1970   *It's Just A Matter of Time*
My Love
Don't Keep Me Hangin' On
Endlessly

1971   *Empty Arms*
Bright Lights, Big City
Here Comes Honey Again

HONKY TONK BLUES

The Billboard chart positions of Hank Williams' Top Twenty singles

1949	*Lovesick Blues*	1
1949	*Wedding Bells*	2
1949	*Mind Your Own Business*	6
1949	*You're Gonna Change*	4
1949	*Lost Highway*	12
1949	*My Bucket's Got A Hole In It*	2
1950	*I Just Don't Like This Kind Of Livin'*	5
1950	*Long Gone Lonesome Blues*	1
1950	*Why Don't You Love Me*	1
1950	*Why Should We Try Anymore*	9
1950	*Moaning The Blues*	2
1951	*Cold Cold Heart*	2
1951	*Dear John*	10
1951	*Howlin' At The Moon*	4
1951	*I Can't Help It*	6
1951	*Hey Good Lookin'*	2
1951	*Crazy Heart*	7
1951	*Baby We're Really In Love*	8
1952	*Honky Tonk Blues*	7
1952	*Half As Much*	2
1952	*Jambalaya*	1
1952	*Settin' The Woods On Fire*	5
1952	*I'll Never Get Out Of This World Alive*	1
1953	*Kaw-Liga*	1
1953	*Your Cheatin' Heart*	2
1953	*Take These Chains From My Heart*	1
1953	*I Won't Be Home No More*	4
1953	*Weary Blues From Waitin'*	7

Hank Williams with Minnie Pearl and the Drifting Cowboys

Additional facts

At the time of his death – New Year's Day 1953 – Hank Williams' current single was "I'll Never Get Out Of This World Alive."

Despite several of his singles passing the million sales mark, Williams only ever had one pop chart hit in the USA – with "Jambalaya," which climbed to No. 23 during 1952.

Williams recorded several sides as Luke The Drifter but failed to chart with any of them. But his son, Hank Jr, later recorded as Luke The Drifter Jr and fared rather better, enjoying several minor hits plus a top twenty entry with "Custody" (1969).

On several occasions, both A and B sides of Williams' singles appeared in the charts individually, "You're Gonna Change" being backed with "Lost Highway," "Cold Cold Heart" with "Dear John," "Howlin' At The Moon" with "I Can't Help It," and "Kaw-Liga" with "Your Cheatin' Heart."

HONKY TONKIN'

Eight great Country Music nightspots

Gilley's
Pasadena, Texas

Mickey Gilley and Sherwood Cryer's club has become a Texas institution and is known throughout the world since its appearance in the film *Urban Cowboy*, which starred John Travolta and the club's mechanical bull. Gilley's has grown in size with its popularity, is now big enough to herd cattle through, and has a rodeo stadium out back. *Urban Cowboy* did turn the club into a tourist trap for a while but caused no long-term damage – it still draws the same blue-collar Country fans and remains one of the best places in the world to see hard-core Country heroes like George Jones and John Anderson. Like all the best honky tonks, a lot of beer is consumed at Gilley's and the place can get a little rowdy late at night.

Billy Bob's Texas
Fort Worth, Texas

Now claiming to be the "world's largest nightspot," Billy Bob Barnett's club covers 100,000 square feet, holds six thousand people and features a huge dancefloor, an indoor rodeo arena with real bulls, and 42 bar stations. Billy Bob's, like Gilley's, is very successful and can afford to book the biggest names in Country music, though the stars have to face a notoriously tough and hard-to-please audience of Fort Worth cowboys.

The Grapevine Opry
Grapevine, Texas

The Grapevine Opry is the very antithesis of Gilley's and Billy Bob's, as their PR lady explains: "When Chisai Childs created the Grapevine Opry she kept the music and the fun but left out the beer, the booze, the smoke and the fights. The result is clean family entertainment where you can take the kids, minister or grandmothers, and have a good time." Grapevine is situated midway between Dallas and Fort Worth and the Opry offers two entertaining shows every Saturday night.

Jay's Lounge and Cockpit
Cankton, Louisiana

An atmospheric honky tonk on a lonely stretch of Highway 93 near Cankton, which is recommended for people who enjoy uninhibited dancing and the music of bands like Asleep At The Wheel. Next door is the cockpit where Mexican and Cajun farmworkers have been gambling over fighting cocks for generations. $1 gets you in, but strangers aren't particularly welcome. Musicians playing in the lounge usually end their evening eating Cock Gumbo.

82

The Longhorn Ballroom
Fort Worth, Texas

One of the few surviving traditional Texas dancehalls, the building began life as "Bob Wills' Ranch House" and then went through a variety of name changes and owners – including Jack Ruby, who later killed Lee Harvey Oswald – before becoming the Longhorn Ballroom in 1957, under the successful management of Dewey Groom, who has subsequently booked almost every Country star of note.

The Palomino
North Hollywood, California

The Palomino is just down the road from Nudies, the famous rodeo tailors, and close to the homes of Ricky Nelson and Phil Everly. While most clubs in Greater Los Angeles have relatively short lives, the Pal is now in its fourth decade and still under the watchful eye of owner Tommy Thomas, who's one of the most respected club bosses in America. The Palomino is a popular venue with musicians as well as Country fans and there are often more stars in the audience than on stage. The club has played host to some classic gigs from the likes of Linda Ronstadt, Elvis Costello and John Stewart.

The Lone Star Cafe
New York, New York

Manhattan's version of a Texas honky tonk is more like the set of a Randolph Scott movie. A rip-roaring success since Billy Swan's opening night in 1977, the club features rough and ready Country artists like Kinky Friedman and Ray Wylie Hubbard plus gut-bucket rhythm and blues acts. The seating arrangements are bizarre; drinkers perched on barstools get a better view than customers paying cover charges to sit at small tables, but nobody seems to care – the atmosphere and the chance to pretend you're in Texas is what most people come for.

Cain's Ballroom
Tulsa, Oklahoma

Cain's Ballroom has been presenting live musical entertainment since the thirties and is the only venue in America which can claim to have featured Bob Wills and his Texas Playboys, Hank Williams *and* the Sex Pistols in their respective heydays! Cain's is preserved today in its original non-air-conditioned splendor as an historic site, and portraits of the C&W greats still line the walls, though you're actually more likely to find young heavy metal musicians on stage than contemporary Country line-ups.

Cain's Ballroom

IF YOU'VE GOT THE MONEY, I'VE GOT THE TIME

The highest-paid Country entertainers in Las Vegas

The fees paid to Country stars tend to be closely guarded secrets, but information occasionally leaks out. In 1983 the *American Almanac of Jobs and Salaries* revealed that six of the top ten money-earners in Las Vegas are Country entertainers and that Dolly Parton commands the highest fee of all performers, including Frank Sinatra and Diana Ross. The following are weekly salaries:

Dolly Parton	**$350,000**	Tom Jones	**$200,000**
Kenny Rogers	**$250,000**	Glen Campbell	**$200,000**
Willie Nelson	**$200,000**	Tammy Wynette	**$150,000**

Dolly Parton

I GOT STRIPES

Country stars who have spent time behind bars

Johnny Cash

Though Johnny's famed for his prison concerts, his actual stays behind bars have proved of short duration. In October 1965, he received a 30-day suspended sentence after being picked up by the El Paso narcotics squad, and during 1966 he was given board and lodging for one night by a local jail when he was spotted apparently on a flower-picking spree in the early hours of the morning.

David Allan Coe

A jail-hardened toughie with a yen for poetry, Coe – also known as The Mysterious Rhinestone Cowboy – is said to have killed a fellow inmate at Ohio State Penitentiary after being threatened with a knife. His first album was predictably titled "Penitentiary Blues."

Spade Cooley

One-time King of Western Swing and a Hollywood personality, Spade had his career brought to a halt when he was imprisoned for slaying his wife, Ella Mae. Released in November 1969, he attempted to show that no enmity existed between himself and the law by playing a sheriff's benefit concert that very day. But he suffered a heart attack during the show and never recovered.

Freddy Fender

Some years before his "Before The Next Teardrop Falls" headed the US pop charts, his life had more in common with a line from "Me And Bobby McGee," Freddy getting busted down in Baton Rouge, after being turned in by a paroled informer. Sentenced to imprisonment for possession of marijuana, he continued his singing career while behind bars and even cut records in the confines of Angola State Penitentiary.

Freddy Fender

Merle Haggard

A tearaway in his younger days, Merle got involved in numerous small-time crimes and was in and out of reform schools, institutions and local jails. Then in '57, when Merle was 20, came the big one – he was sentenced on a one to ten stretch after being convicted of attempted burglary. But he was free again in 1960, having decided to mend his ways following a spell in solitary confinement just a few cells away from San Quentin's most famous prisoner, Caryl Chessman.

Merle Haggard

Aunt Mollie Jackson

One of the great historical figures of Country music, Aunt Mollie was jailed at the age of 10 for being involved in trade union activities. Later, the singer was blacklisted throughout Kentucky because of her beliefs and was forced to move to New York in order to find work.

Willie Nelson

Willie was jailed for several hours in the Bahamas after a customs official opened up the Nelson suitcase and discovered a package of suspicious substance inside the Texan's packed jeans. "It cost me $700 to get out," he later complained, though he claims that his brief spell of imprisonment was made tolerable thanks to an ample supply of beer, sneaked into the jail by Hank Cochran. Later, Willie was deported and asked never to return.

Johnny Rodriguez

Another who fell foul of the law at an early age, Johnny collected an interesting tally of minor offenses, including the barbecuing of a goat that he and his friends had stolen. But the kind-hearted Texas Ranger who arrested him for the misdemeanor also found the young Chicano his first job in Country music, thus setting him on the straight and narrow.

Johnny Rodriguez

I LOVE THE SOUND OF A WHISTLE

Boxcar Willie's favorite train songs

Boxcar Willie comments:

"Wabash Cannonball" is everybody's favorite train song, while "Hobo's Meditation" is another of my high favorites. Each train song has its own personality and, when you come down to it, it's hard to put them in any sort of order. "Fireball Mail" has fond memories though – I recorded that one with Roy Acuff for Elektra. Then there's a song of my own I wrote recently, it's called "Old Iron Trail" and I hope it's destined to become a classic someday. I love train songs – I could name a hundred, I guess, though "Wabash Cannonball" remains my all-time favorite. I have my own railroad museum. It's a traveling museum, going all over America. I have lots of train memorabilia in there – some things that ole Boxcar's collected from thirty-eight countries around the world – things that people have given me, things that people wanted me to have . . . which makes everything three times as valuable in my eyes. Now most of the steam trains have gone and it's all diesel and electric – I guess that's progress. And that's got to happen. I mean, I really enjoy flying the old biplanes – but you can't get very far, very fast, these days.

Wabash Cannonball
I Love The Sound Of A Whistle
Fireball Mail
The Streamline Cannonball
Rock Island Line

The Golden Rocket
The Lord Made A Hobo Out Of Me
Orange Blossom Special
Hobo's Meditation
Waitin' For A Train

IMAGINE THAT

Stars' names and how they originated

Jessie Colter

Buddy Holly and The Crickets

Jessi Colter
Real name Miriam Johnson. She took her name from a great-great-uncle, Jesse Colter, who had been a notorious outlaw and counterfeiter.

The Crickets
Buddy Holly and his group chose their name by looking through a dictionary for an insect which "sang." They settled for cricket because it chirped.

Freddy Fender
He was born Baldema Huerta but changed his name to that of his guitar brand. On the Bandstand TV Show, he told Dick Clark: "It was easier for a gringo to drop a dime in the jukebox if the artist's name was Freddy Fender."

Crystal Gayle
Real name Brenda Gail Webb. Big sister Loretta Lynn gave her a nickname after the Krystal hamburger chain.

Bobbie Gentry

Real name Roberta Streeter. She changed her name after seeing Charlton Heston and Jennifer Jones in the movie *Ruby Gentry*.

Grandpa Jones

Real name Louis Marshall Jones. In his early twenties, Louis was singing on a radio show when a listener wrote in and asked about "the new singer with the old voice." Soon afterwards he adopted the Grandpa Jones character and for stage shows dressed up as an old man.

C.W. McCall

Bill Fries, the creative director of an advertising agency, invented the truck-driving character of "C.W. McCall" for commercials to advertise Old Home Bread, was unable to find an actor to read the lyrics to his satisfaction, so used his own voice, and then, at the suggestion of a friend in the music industry, began making recitation records as C.W. McCall and subsequently scored hits, including "Convoy."

T.G. Sheppard

Real name Bill Browder. "One night I sat down and made up a fictitious name, T.G. Sheppard, and put everything into that name that I wanted to be as an entertainer. The initials were just initials, but I've been tagged 'The Good Sheppard' and that's kinda stuck."

The Statler Brothers

Their name came from a box of paper tissues which they saw in a hotel room. "We could just as easily have been named the Kleenex Brothers," recalls Harold Reid.

Conway Twitty

Real name Harold Lloyd Jenkins, he took his performing name from two towns near his home – Conway, Arkansas and Twitty, Texas.

Kitty Wells

Real name Muriel Deason. She changed her name at the suggestion of her husband, Johnny Wright, after the Carter Family song "Sweet Kitty Wells."

Kitty Wells with her husband Johnny Wright

Tammy Wynette

Real name Virginia Wynette Pugh. Nashville producer Billy Sherrill loved the sound of her voice but hated the name – "You look like a Tammy to me," he told her.

I'M GONNA WRITE A SONG

The Songwriters Hall of Fame

Bill Monroe

The Nashville Songwriters Association established a Songwriters Hall of Fame in 1970 to honor writers deemed to have made major contributions to the world of Country music. Those so far honored are:

1970   Gene Autry, Johnny Bond, Albert Brumley, A.P. Carter, Ted Daffan, Vernon Dalhart, Rex Griffin, Stuart Hamblen, Pee Wee King, Vic McAlpin, Bob Miller, Leon Payne, Jimmie Rodgers, Fred Rose, Redd Stewart, Floyd Tillman, Merle Travis, Ernest Tubb, Cindy Walker, Hank Williams, Bob Wills

1971   Smiley Burnette, Jenny Lou Carson, Wilf Carter, Zeke Clements, Jimmie Davis, Alton Delmore, Rabon Delmore, Al Dexter, Vaughn Horton, Bradley Kincaid, Bill Monroe, Bob Nolan, Tex Owens, Tex Ritter, Carson J. Robison, Tim Spencer, Wiley Walker, Gene Sullivan, Jimmy Wakely, Scotty Wiseman

1972   Boudleaux and Felice Bryant, Jack Rhodes, Don Robertson, Lefty Frizzell

1973	Jack Clement, Don Gibson, Harlan Howard, Roger Miller, Ed Nelson Jr, Steve Nelson, Willie Nelson
1974	Hank Cochran
1975	Marty Robbins, Wayne Walker, Danny Dill, Eddie Miller, Bill Anderson, Marijohn Wilkin
1976	Carl Belew, Dallas Frazier, John D. Loudermilk, Moon Mullican, Curly Putnam, Mel Tillis
1977	Woody Guthrie, Johnny Cash, Merle Haggard, Kris Kristofferson
1978	Joe Allison, Tom T. Hall, Hank Snow, Don Wayne
1979	Rev. Thomas A. Dorsey, Louvin Brothers, Elsie McWilliams, Joe South
1980	Huddie Ledbetter, Mickey Newbury, Ben Peters, Ray Stevens
1981	Bobby Braddock, Ray Whitley
1982	Chuck Berry, William J. (Billy) Hill
1983	Loretta Lynn, Beasley Smith, W.C. Handy

Tex Ritter and Merle Travis

I TAKE A LOT OF PRIDE IN WHAT I AM

Black music artists who have made Country albums

A black musician, Deford Bailey, was the first man to play on the Grand Ole Opry. Jimmie Rodgers learnt his music from black railroad workers and frequently used black sidemen on his records, while Hank Williams was heavily influenced by a black street singer named Tee-Tot. These days, Charley Pride ranks among the most popular Country artists in America, while others, like Linda Martel and Stoney Edwards, have done much to dispel the fallacy that Country is purely white man's music. But there are still some black people who have no time for Nashville traditions. "If the guy who writes about me is a Charley Pride fan," said Archie Bell, the black Texan who leads the soulful Drells, "then he's got no business writing about me. How can you write about dogs when you raise horses?"

Every field has its share of awkward customers.

Ray Charles	*Modern Sounds In Country And Western* (ABC US/HMV UK)
	Modern Sounds In Country And Western Vol.2 (ABC US/HMV UK)
	Love Country Style (ABC US/Probe UK)
	Wish You Were Here Tonight (Columbia US/CBS UK)
Millie Jackson	*Just A Lil Bit Country* (Spring US/Polydor UK)
Dobie Gray	*Drift Away* (MCA)
Esther Phillips	*Reflections Of Country And Western Greats* (Lenox US/Ember UK)
Joe Tex	*Soul Country* (Atlantic)
O.B. McClinton	*Obie From Senatobie* (Enterprise US)
	Live At Randy's Rodeo (Enterprise US)
B.B. King	*Love Me Tender* (MCA)
Bettye Swann	*Don't Touch Me* (Capitol US)
Tina Turner	*The Country Of Tina Turner* (UA)
Lou Rawls	*When The Night Comes* (Epic)
Memphis Slim	*Going Back To Tennessee* (Barclay UK)
Nat King Cole	*Ramblin' Rose* (Capitol)
Gatemouth Brown	*Blackjack* (Music Is Medicine US)
Bobby Womack	*B.W. Goes C & W* (UA)
Joe Simon	*Simon Country* (Spring US/Polydor UK)

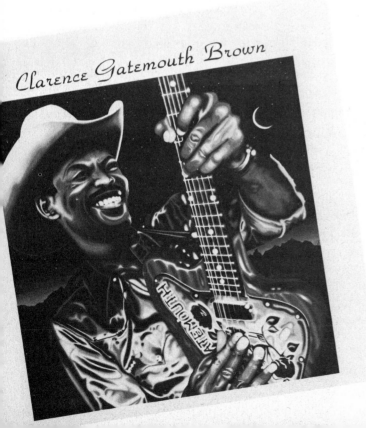

I'VE BEEN EVERYWHERE

The firsts of George Hamilton IV

George Hamilton has a conformist image with some people because of his short hair and always neat appearance, but beneath that "Gentleman George" exterior there lurks a non-conformist musical rebel! George is one of Country music's most important pioneers, which was recognized in 1975 when *Billboard* presented him with the magazine's "Trendsetter" award for being the first American Country artist to perform in the Soviet Union. He's also one of Country's most traveled performers and has earned the title "The Ambassador Of Country Music." Here's George's list of some of his firsts:

1956   A million-seller with his first record, the pop hit "A Rose And A Baby Ruth."

1960   George turned his back on a promising future as a pop singer and returned to his first love, Country music. This was a first for an established pop artist with a track record of Top 40 hits to "go Country." Others followed suit, including Jerry Lee Lewis, Conway Twitty, Billy "Crash" Craddock and others.

1963   George helped give birth to the "folk Country" movement in Nashville with his recording of "Abilene."

1965   George became the first Nashville-based act to record extensively the songs of Gordon Lightfoot. He's subsequently recorded over two dozen of his songs.

1967   He became the first artist to take a Joni Mitchell song, "Urge For Going," into the top ten of the Country charts.

1969   The first American Country artist to record an entire LP of Canadian songs. Also the year that George appeared at the first International Festival of Country Music in London. He's subsequently appeared at more of these festivals than anyone else. He later performed and compered the first International Country Festivals in Sweden (1976), Finland (1977), Holland and Norway (1978), Germany (1979), and Paris and Zurich (1980).

1970   The first American Country artist to record an album in England using all English songs and personnel.

1972   Became the first American Country singer to have his own TV series in England. He's now done eight BBC TV series

1974   George became the first American Country artist to give a concert tour behind the Iron Curtain. He performed in Russia and Czechoslovakia.

1979   He appeared in England's first Country music summer season show – three months in concert at the Winter Gardens Theatre in Blackpool.

1982   He completed the longest ever British Country music tour, visiting sixty cities in England, Scotland and Wales. Still keeping up the momentum, George becomes the first US Country artist to record an album behind the Iron Curtain.

George Hamilton IV

I'VE BEEN WAITING FOR YOU ALL OF MY LIFE

America's rarest Country singles and their value

Over $700.00	Jimmie Rodgers *Blue Yodel No. 12* (Victor 18-6000) 78 rpm – a picture disc that was released in 1933
Over $300.00	Elvis Presley *That's All Right Mama* (Sun 209) 45 rpm Elvis Presley *Milkcow Blues Boogie* (Sun 215) 45 rpm
Over $200.00	Elvis Presley *Good Rockin' Tonight* (Sun 210) 45 rpm Elvis Presley *I'm Left, You're Right, She's Gone* (Sun 217) 45 rpm
Over $150.00	Charlie Feathers *I've Been Deceived* (Sun 503) 45 rpm Charlie Feathers *I've Been Deceived* (Flip 503) 45 rpm Hank Williams *Calling You* (Sterling 201) 78 rpm Elvis Presley *Mystery Train* (Sun 223) 45 rpm
Over $100.00	Hank Williams *Wealth Won't Save Your Soul* (Sterling 204) 78 rpm Ernest Tubb *The Passing Of Jimmie Rodgers* (Bluebird 6693) 78 rpm Fort Worth Doughboys *Nancy Jane* (Bluebird 5257) 78 rpm Charlie Feathers *Defrost Your Heart* (Sun 231) 45 rpm Carl Perkins *Movie Magg* (Flip 501) 45 rpm Bill Taylor and Smokey Jo *Split Personality* (Flip 502) 45 rpm
Over $80.00	Hardrock Gunter *Fallen Angel* (Sun 201) 45 rpm Cochran Brothers *Tired And Sleepy* (Ekko 3001) 45 rpm Ernest Tubb *The T.B. Is Whipping Me* (Bluebird 7000) 78 rpm Hank Williams *I Don't Care* (Sterling 208) 78 rpm

The Fort Worth Doughboys disc on Bluebird 5257 was the first release by Bob Wills and Milton Brown, while Sterling 201 was Hank Williams' debut single.

Few "straight" Country records command high prices in Britain – but here are a few of the more collectible items, mainly rockabilly issues, that could be of interest to Country fans. All are UK-released 45 rpm singles.

Over £100	Jackie Lee Cochran *Mama Don't You Think I Know* (Brunswick 05669)
	Werly Fairburn And The Delta Boys *All The Time* (London HLC 8349)
	Mac Curtis *You Ain't Treating Me Right* (Parlophone R4279)
	Peanuts Wilson *Cast Iron Arm* (Coral Q72302)
Over £60	Moon Mullican and Boyd Bennett *Seven Nights To Rock* (Parlophone MSP 6254)
Over £40	Webb Pierce *Teenage Boogie* (Brunswick 05630)
	Buddy Holly *Blue Days, Black Nights* (Brunswick 05581)
	Johnny Burnette Trio *Tear It Up* (Coral Q72177)
Over £30	Brenda Lee *I'm Gonna Lassoo Santa Claus* (Brunswick 05628)
	Johnny Burnette Trio *Lonesome Train* (Coral Q72227)
	Eager Beaver Baby (Coral Q72283)
	Elvis Presley *Rip It Up* (HMV POP 305)
	Mystery Train (HMV POP 295)
	Blue Suede Shoes (HMV 7M405)
Over £20	Elvis Presley *Heartbreak Hotel* (HMV 7M385)
	Love Me Tender (HMV POP 253)
	Paralyzed (HMV POP 378)
	Too Much (HMV POP 330)
	My Baby Left Me (HMV 7M424)
	Brenda Lee *Dynamite* (Brunswick 05685)
	Ain't That Love (Brunswick 05720)
	Little Jonah (Brunswick 05755)
	Warner Mack *Rock A Chicka* (Brunswick 05728)
	Carl Perkins *Blue Suede Shoes* (London HLU 8271)
	Johnny Faire *Bertha Lou* (London HLU 8569)
	Johnny Cash *I Walk The Line* (London HL 8358)

All values given are for records in mint or near mint condition.

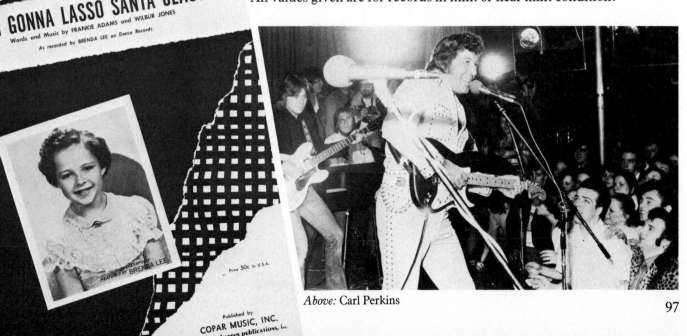

Above: Carl Perkins

I'VE GOT A WINNER IN YOU

Sand Tarts: Don Williams' favorite recipe

Ingredients: 2 sticks of butter, 6 tablespoons of powdered sugar, 2 cups of flour, 1½ teaspoons vanilla and 1 cup of chopped pecan nuts.

1   Cream sugar and butter (if you use an electric mixer the cookies turn out much lighter).
2   Add flour and vanilla, mix well, and add nuts.
3   Roll small amount of dough (1½ inches in diameter) into a ball and place on a greased tray.
4   Bake for 21 minutes in a pre-heated oven (350°, gas mark 4).
5   Immediately upon removal from oven, roll each cookie in powdered sugar.

I WANT TO PLAY MY HORN ON THE GRAND OLE OPRY

Milestones in the history of WSM Incorporated, owners of the Grand Ole Opry and Opryland

October 5, 1925	The first broadcast over the National Life and Accident Insurance Company's new radio station, WSM. The call letters stood for "We Shield Millions."
November 28, 1925	The WSM Barn Dance (forerunner of the Grand Ole Opry) is launched. The first program is introduced by George D. Hay and features an 80-year-old fiddle player named Uncle Jimmy Thompson, accompanied by his niece, Mrs Eva Thompson Jones, on piano.
1927	The WSM Barn Dance becomes known as the Grand Ole Opry. Early cast members include Dr Humphrey Bate and his Possum Hunters, Uncle Dave Macon and the first black star in Country music's history, Deford Bailey.
1932	WSM is awarded a clear channel at 650 kilocycles and also receives permission from the Federal Radio Commission to increase its power from 5000 to 50,000 watts. The Saturday night Grand Ole Opry could now be heard by a huge radio audience in several states.
1937	Roy Acuff joins the cast of the Grand Ole Opry, beginning an era where solo singers rather than groups are the most popular performers. Within a few years, Acuff became the artist most closely associated with the Opry.
1943	After a variety of temporary homes, including the Dixie Tabernacle and the War Memorial Auditorium, the Grand Ole Opry finds a permanent home at the Ryman Auditorium in downtown Nashville. It stayed there for 31 years.
September 30, 1950	WSM brings Nashville its first TV station, WSM-TV, an NBC affiliate.
1955	Grand Ole Opry, WSM's first networked show, is telecast on ABC-TV.

1965	WSM-TV brings the first color programming to Nashville.
1966	WSM handles the first network telecast of the Country Music Association Awards Show from the Ryman Auditorium.
June 30, 1970	The official groundbreaking for the Opryland USA musical entertainment theme park.
May 27, 1972	Opening of Opryland USA.
March 16, 1974	The Grand Ole Opry moves into the new Grand Ole Opry House at the Opryland entertainment complex. The new theater lacked the down-home atmosphere of the old Ryman building but most of the artists were pleased to move because of the much improved back-stage facilities.
1974	Opryland Productions television and commercial production operation goes into business in the Grand Ole Opry House.
November 1977	The Opryland Hotel, Tennessee's largest convention hotel property, opens.
March 4, 1978	The Grand Ole Opry is televised live over the Public Broadcasting Service.
September 1980	WSM forms Opryland Radio Productions to produce and market syndicated and network radio programming.
March 11, 1981	The NLT Corp., parent company of WSM Inc., announces plans for the sale of WSM-TV to make way for WSM's entry into satellite and cable television programming.
September 12, 1981	"Nashville Alive," the first live cable television series to be telecast from Nashville, premieres from the Stagedoor Lounge of the Opryland Hotel and is telecast via WTBS from Atlanta.
December 8, 1981	WSM and Associated Press announce the Music Country Network, an overnight satellite radio network, with WSM-AM as the flagship station.
March 7, 1983	Launch of the Nashville Network, an 18-hour-a-day Country-orientated cable TV service. The five-hour live debut show involves dozens of Country stars in six major American cities.

I WAS COUNTRY WHEN COUNTRY WASN'T COOL

CMA awards . . .

The Country Music Association's annual awards are the most prestigious made in the Country music industry. The winners are chosen by the combined votes of all the CMA members – some 7000 professionals who earn at least a third of their income from Country music. All categories except two – Song of the Year and the Horizon Award – are selected strictly by the votes of CMA members. The Song of the Year winner is determined by a combination of total membership votes and a song's appearance on the national charts of leading trade magazines. Nominations for the Horizon Award are made by CMA board members, then submitted to the entire membership during the second and third rounds of voting. The winners are announced at the CMA Awards Ceremony, held at the Grand Ole Opry House in Nashville each October.

8	**Alabama**	Entertainer of the Year 1982, 1983 Vocal Group of the Year 1981, 1982, 1983 Instrumental Group of the Year, 1981, 1982 Album of the Year *The Closer You Get* (RCA) 1983
8	**Loretta Lynn**	Entertainer of the Year 1972 Female Vocalist of the Year 1967, 1972, 1973 Vocal Duo of the Year (with Conway Twitty) 1972, 1973, 1974, 1975
8	**The Statler Brothers**	Vocal Group of the Year 1972, 1973, 1974, 1975, 1976, 1977, 1979, 1980
7	**Roy Clark**	Entertainer of the Year 1973 Instrumentalist of the Year 1977, 1978, 1980 Instrumental Group of the Year (with Buck Trent) 1975, 1976 Comedian of the Year 1970
7	**Ronnie Milsap**	Entertainer of the Year 1977 Male Vocalist of the Year 1974, 1976, 1977 Album of the Year *A Legend In My Time* (RCA) 1975, *Ronnie Milsap Live* (RCA) 1977, *It Was Almost Like A Song* (RCA) 1978

7	**Willie Nelson**	Entertainer of the Year 1979 Single of the Year *Good Hearted Woman* (with Waylon Jennings) (RCA) 1976, *Always On My Mind* (Columbia) 1982 Album of the Year *Wanted: The Outlaws* (with Waylon Jennings, Jessi Colter and Tompall) (RCA) 1976, *Always On My Mind* (Columbia) 1982 Vocal Duo of the Year (with Waylon Jennings) 1976, (with Merle Haggard) 1983
6	**Johnny Cash**	Entertainer of the Year 1969 Male Vocalist of the Year 1969 Single of the Year *A Boy Named Sue* (Columbia) 1969 Album of the Year *Johnny Cash At Folsom Prison* (Columbia) 1968, *Johnny Cash At San Quentin* (Columbia) 1969 Vocal Group of the Year (with June Carter) 1969
6	**Danny Davis and The Nashville Brass**	Instrumental Group of the Year 1969, 1970, 1971, 1972, 1973, 1974
6	**Dolly Parton**	Entertainer of the Year 1978 Female Vocalist of the Year 1975, 1976 Vocal Duo of the Year (with Porter Wagoner) 1970, 1971 Vocal Group of the Year (with Porter Wagoner) 1968
6	**Merle Haggard**	Entertainer of the Year 1970 Male Vocalist of the Year 1970 Single of the Year *Okie From Muskogee* (Capitol) 1970 Album of the Year *Okie From Muskogee* (Capitol) 1970, *Let Me Tell You About A Song* (Capitol) 1972 Vocal Duo of the Year (with Willie Nelson) 1983
6	**Chet Atkins**	Instrumentalist of the Year 1967, 1968, 1969, 1981, 1982, 1983
5	**Charlie Rich**	Entertainer of the Year 1974 Male Vocalist of the Year 1973 Single of the Year *Behind Closed Doors* (Epic) 1973 Album of the Year *Behind Closed Doors* (Epic) 1973, *A Very Special Love Song* (Epic) 1974
5	**Kenny Rogers**	Male Vocalist of the Year 1979 Single of the Year *Lucille* (United Artists) 1977 Album of the Year *The Gambler* (United Artists) 1979 Vocal Duo of the Year (with Dottie West) 1978, 1979
4	**Waylon Jennings**	Male Vocalist of the Year 1975 Single of the Year *Good Hearted Woman* (with Willie Nelson) (RCA) 1976 Album of the Year *Wanted: The Outlaws* (with Willie Nelson, Jessi Colter and Tompall) (RCA) 1976 Vocal Duo of the Year (with Willie Nelson) 1976
4	**Barbara Mandrell**	Entertainer of the Year 1980, 1981 Female Vocalist of the Year 1979, 1981
4	**Conway Twitty**	Vocal Duo of the Year (with Loretta Lynn) 1972, 1973, 1974, 1975

Barbara Mandrell and Mac Davis at the 1981
CMA Awards Show

3	**Charlie Daniels Band**	Single of the Year *The Devil Went Down To Georgia* (Epic) 1979 Instrumental Group of the Year 1979, 1980
3	**Jack Greene**	Male Vocalist of the Year 1967 Single of the Year *There Goes My Everything* (Decca) 1967 Album of the Year *There Goes My Everything* (Decca) 1967
3	**George Jones**	Male Vocalist of the Year 1980, 1981 Single of the Year *He Stopped Loving Her Today* (Epic) 1980
3	**Charley Pride**	Entertainer of the Year 1971 Male Vocalist of the Year 1971, 1972
3	**Porter Wagoner**	Vocal Group of the Year (with Dolly Parton) 1968 Vocal Duo of the Year (with Dolly Parton) 1970, 1971
3	**Tammy Wynette**	Female Vocalist of the Year 1968, 1969, 1970

. . . and CMA highlights

Highlights of the CMA's contribution to the growth of Country music

For over 25 years, the Country Music Association has worked to promote the growth and understanding of Country music around the world. Since its founding in 1958, the CMA's membership has grown from the original 200 to more than 7000 Country music professionals. It was the first trade organization ever formed to promote a type of music.

Country Music Month

– an annual international celebration held each October which is recognized by the American President, state governors and numerous foreign heads of state.

The CMA Awards	– annual awards presentation to top Country acts, as voted by CMA members since 1967. The CMA Awards show has been on national television in the US since 1968.
Fan Fair	– now one of the world's biggest Country music celebrations. Co-sponsored with the Grand Ole Opry, the International Country Music Fan Fair attracts thousands of fans from around the world to Nashville to meet their favorite stars, see exhibits and shows.
Close-Up Magazine	– a monthly publication giving information to all members.
CMA International Office	– the growth of the Country music industry necessitated the opening of a European office in London.
DJ Awards	– given each year to the top American Country music disc jockeys in small, medium and large market areas.
Talent Buyers Seminar	– held to promote the use of Country acts in fairs, auditoriums, parks and theaters.
Information source	– the CMA is recognized throughout the music industry as the definitive source on the growth of Country music, past and future.
Country Music Hall Of Fame	– honoring Country music greats, and building the Country Music Hall Of Fame Museum in Nashville.
Legislative support	– to aid bills that benefit the music industry.

Ronald Reagan and galaxy of Country stars celebrating the CMA 25th birthday

A LEGEND IN MY TIME

The hits of Studio B – Nashville's most famous studio

RCA's Studio B is probably the most famous and successful studio in the history of the Nashville recording industry. It was built in 1957 at the insistence of Chet Atkins, the newly appointed Manager of Operations for RCA Victor in Nashville, who was sure that RCA needed to own a separate studio rather than continue sharing space with the Methodist Radio and Television Foundation at a building on McGavock Street. The new studio, built at a cost of $39,515 and located at the junction of the streets now known as Roy Acuff Place and Music Square West, was very successful and used by other record companies whenever there was time between the RCA acts. Elvis Presley, who cut over 100 tracks there, Waylon Jennings, Hank Snow and Jim Reeves were among the artists who used the building frequently. Studio B was closely associated with the smooth "Nashville Sound" and featured hundreds of sessions by a small and very talented group of musicians – Harold Bradley (electric bass, rhythm guitar), Pete Drake (pedal steel guitar), Floyd Cramer (piano), Ray Edenton (rhythm guitar), Grady Martin (lead and rhythm guitar), Charlie McCoy (harmonica), Hargus "Pig" Robbins (piano), Tommy Jackson (fiddle), Bob Moore (upright bass) and Buddy Harmon (drums) – who between them played on almost every Nashville Country hit of the late fifties and sixties. RCA closed Studio B in 1977, but the building was then acquired by the Country Music Foundation who opened it to the public as a historic site. Today visitors receive a guided tour and learn about the art of recording and the history of the studio.

A Selective List

Eddy Arnold	*You Slipped A Little Heartache In On Me*
	Tennessee Stud
Chet Atkins	*Country Gentleman*
Bobby Bare	*Detroit City*
Blackwood Brothers Quartet	*Wonderful Time Up There*
Jim Ed Brown	*Southern Loving*
The Browns	*The Three Bells*

Archie Campbell	*Trouble In Amen Corner*
Floyd Cramer	*Last Date*
Dave and Sugar	*Queen Of The Silver Dollar*
Skeeter Davis	*The End Of The World*
Jimmy Driftwood	*Battle Of New Orleans*
Everly Brothers	*Cathy's Clown*
Don Gibson	*A Legend In My Time*
Waylon Jennings	*I'm A Ramblin' Man*
	Brown Eyed Handsome Man
Hank Locklin	*Please Help Me I'm Falling*
Ronnie Milsap	*Who'll Turn Out The Lights*
Willie Nelson	*Bloody Mary Morning*
Dolly Parton	*Love Is Like A Butterfly*
	The Seeker
Elvis Presley	*Stuck On You*
	A Fool Such As I
	Crying In The Chapel
	Follow That Dream
Charley Pride	*Kiss An Angel Good Morning*
Boots Randolph	*Yakety Sax*
Jerry Reed	*Alabama Wild Man*
Jim Reeves	*Welcome To My World*
Johnny Rodriguez	*Dance With Me*
Hank Snow	*I've Been Everywhere*
The Statesmen	*I'll Fly Away*
Porter Wagoner	*Cold Dark Waters*
Dottie West	*Here Comes My Baby*
Del Wood	*Alabama Jubilee*

Chet Atkins

Studio B

LET'S GET TOGETHER

Singers or groups of singers who have appeared on record with George Jones

Tammy Wynette
Waylon Jennings
James Taylor
Emmylou Harris
Linda Ronstadt
Willie Nelson
Johnny Paycheck
Elvis Costello
Pop and Mavis Staples
Ray Sawyer and Dennis Locorriere

Melba Montgomery
Gene Pitney
The Oak Ridge Boys
The Jordanaires
Nashville Edition
Brenda Carter
Margie Singleton
Ernest Tubb
Virginia Spurlock
Barbara Mandrell
Ray Charles

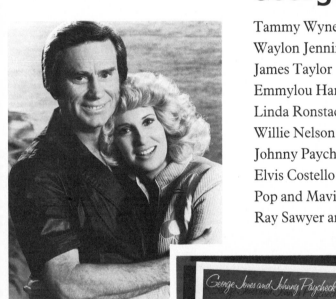

With Tammy Wynette

MY NAME IS MUD

Singers who have recorded under a pseudonym

George Jones	*(Thumper Jones)*
Freddy Fender	*(Scotty Wayne)*
Hank Williams Jr	*(Luke The Drifter Jr)*
Hank Williams	*(Luke The Drifter)*
Johnny Paycheck	*(Donny Young)*
Ernie Ashworth	*(Billy Worth)*
Ferlin Husky	*(Simon Crum/Terry Preston)*
T.G. Sheppard	*(Brian Stacey)*
Sheb Wooley	*(Ben Colder)*
Gene Autry	*(Overton Hatfield)*
Jerry Lee Lewis	*(The Hawk)*
Buck Owens	*(Corky Jones)*
Charlie Rich	*(Bobby Sheridan)*
John D. Loudermilk	*(Ebe Sneezer)*
Jerry Ellis	*(Orion)*
Jerry Naylor	*(Jackie Garrard)*

Orion (Jerry Ellis) and Orion's bus

Charlie Rich

Though many Country singers have recorded under other names, none has come remotely near to the number of aliases adopted by Vernon Dalhart, maker of *The Prisoner's Song*, the first Country record to sell over one million copies. He recorded under at least one hundred different names, these including: James Ahern, John Albin, Mack Allen, Wolf Ballard, James Belmont, Harry Blake, Harry Britt, Billy Burton, Jeff Calhoun, Jimmy Cannon, Jimmy Cantrell, Ed Clifford, Al Cramer, Al Craver, James Cummings, Frank Dalbert, Frank Dalhart, Vernon Dall, Charles Dalton, Vernon Dell, Hugh Donovan, Joseph Elliot, Frank Evans, Clifford Ford, Jeff Fuller, Jep Fuller, Albert Gordon, Leslie Gray, Francis Harold, David Harris, Harry Harris, Lou Hays, Fern Holmes, Howard Hull, Frank Hutchinson, Joe Kincaid, Fred King, Louis Lane, Hugh Latimer, Hugh Lattimore, Tobe Little, The Lone Star Ranger, Bob Massey, Guy Massey, Bob McAfee, Carlos B. McAfee, Warren Mitchell, George Morbid, Dick Morse, Charles Nelson, Gwyrick O'Hara, Sam Peters, Joseph Smith, Josephus Smith, Cliff Stewart, Edward Stone, Howard Stone, Billy Stuart, Will Terry, The Texas Tenor, Bob Thomas, Al Turner, Allen Turner, Sid Turner, Bill Vernon, Billy Vernon, Herbert Vernon, Val Veteran, Vel Veteran, Tom Watson, Bob White, Bobby White, Robert White, Walter Whitlock, George Woods, the inevitable Mr X and many other assumed identities.

OLD DOGS, CHILDREN & WATERMELON WINE

Tom T. Hall's alcoholic watermelon recipe

1 Find a watermelon patch and steal the biggest watermelon you can find
2 Carve out a plug in the centre and fill the watermelon with about one quart of vodka. Keep the plug
3 Put the plug back tightly in the watermelon
4 Let it sit all day in a cooler packed with ice
5 Pour out the juice and vodka mixture and serve well chilled

A word of CAUTION!

This is a tried and tested recipe by Ole Tom T. himself and he will vouch that it is very potent, so go easy on the amount you drink!

Tom T. Hall

ONE PIECE AT A TIME

The Johnny Cash museum

Hendersonville, Tennessee, which lies a few miles NE of Nashville, is the home of Johnny Cash and his wife June Carter. Drive down the main thoroughfare, part of which is called "Johnny Cash Parkway," and you'll come to the House of Cash, a colonial-style building which houses the Johnny Cash Museum. The curator is Johnny's eldest brother, Roy Cash, and he told us about the most interesting areas and exhibits:

The Inspiration Room — several items used during the filming of *The Gospel Road*, which Johnny and June produced and starred in, including Cash's handwritten script and the robe and crown of thorns worn by Robert Elfstrom, who portrayed Jesus.

Sun Records artifacts — a set of fifties instruments and a Sears Roebuck amplifier. "By today's standards," says Roy, "these musical instruments are primitive and inexpensive. However, these are the instruments used by Johnny and the Tennessee Two, Luther Perkins and Marshall Grant, to record some of their first Sun records, such as 'Hey Porter' and 'I Walk The Line.'"

Gold Discs — "There's room for less than a quarter of his gold records. At the present time Johnny has 45 US gold records and 8 US platinum, besides the countless gold records he's received from abroad. His first gold record came with 'I Walk The Line,' which was recorded in 1956."

Awards — these include the six CMA awards Johnny won in a single year, 1969, also the plaque received in 1980 when he joined the Country Music Hall of Fame. "He's the youngest living member ever inducted," says Roy.

The Cash Cadillac

The Carter Family Area	– Johnny's wife June comes from Country music's first family, the Carter family. The items on display include some of their earliest records and the gold record Mother Maybelle Carter (June's mother) received for her single "Wildwood Flower."
International Items	– the museum offers ample evidence of Johnny's enormous popularity abroad; he has been named as one of the ten best-known people in the world. Johnny's autobiography, *The Man In Black*, has been translated into nine different languages (seven versions are on display), and there are souvenirs from his many foreign trips, including a jacket from his historic visit to Czechoslovakia.
Gifts	– a collection of gifts from fellow Country artists, including Ernest Tubb's stetson, Marty Robbins' shirt, Minnie Pearl's hat, Conway Twitty's briefcase and Roy Acuff's fiddle.
The One Piece At A Time Cadillac	– on display outside the museum, the remarkable car built by an Oklahoma man, Bill Patch, from Cadillac parts dating from 1949 through 1973 and presented to Cash in honor of his 1976 hit recording, "One Piece At A Time."
Childhood	– the Cash family area includes early pictures of Johnny, the iron bed that he slept in and the scales his family weighed cotton with on their 20-acre farm in Dyess, Arkansas.
Bedroom	– includes the Elizabethan four-poster bed that Johnny and June slept in for the first couple of years of their marriage.
Americana	– an original picture of Abraham Lincoln, taken in 1862, a letter written by Andrew Jackson, and some priceless sketches and bronzes by Frederic Remington.

Roy Cash, curator

POP A TOP

Ten crossover hits

Pop stars have often latched onto existing Country music hits in order to further their own careers. Here are a few case histories of songs that made their way from Nashville to top pop charts throughout the world.

Patti Page

Cold Cold Heart

A self-penned Country hit for Hank Williams, it was covered in 1951 by Tony Bennett, who took it to number one in the US pop charts. Later, in 1954, Bennett had another huge success with Hank's "There'll Be No Teardrops Tonight."

Tennessee Waltz

Written by Pee Wee King and Redd Stewart, this chunk of 3/4 virtually took over the US pop charts at the turn of 1950, no less than seven versions of the number gaining places in the top thirty; these were by Patti Page (1), Guy Lombardo (6), Les Paul and Mary Ford (8), Spike Jones (16), Jo Stafford (17), Anita O'Day (24) and the Fontaine Sisters (29).

You Are My Sunshine

If for nothing else, songwriter Jimmy Davis will always be remembered for fashioning "You Are My Sunshine," one of the most popular songs to emerge from Country music during the early forties. Not that Davis is likely to be forgotten, for, apart from writing such other winners as "Nobody's Darlin' But Mine" and "It Makes No Difference Now," he was twice elected Governor of Louisiana and even grabbed an award as the best gospel singer of 1957 – these achievements winning him a place in the Country Music Hall Of Fame. Bing Crosby's recording of "You Are My Sunshine" became an international favorite in 1941, though, oddly enough, it never gained a spot in the upper echelons of the US charts even though Sir Winston Churchill once claimed it as among his favorite songs. Later it became one of the Country classics that went top ten for Ray Charles and also helped provide Mitch Ryder and Johnny and The Hurricanes with more moderate chart positions.

Green, Green Grass Of Home

A Curly Putnam song waxed by fellow Missourians Ferlin Husky and Porter Wagoner, "Green, Green Grass Of Home" eventually broke big on both sides of the Atlantic, in 1966, for Pontypridd's Tom Jones, providing him with his biggest-ever success. Immediately, the Welshman leapt to cover other Country material and in 1967 grabbed two more bestsellers with versions of "Detroit City," a Bobby Bare hit, and "Funny Familiar Forgotten Feelings," a Mickey Newbury composition.

Tobacco Road

A song that bears the same title as a bestselling Erskine Caldwell novel, "Tobacco Road" was the first-ever British top ten (and American top twenty) entry for The Nashville Teens, in 1964. Composed by John D. Loudermilk, a performer who made his TV debut in the company of Tex Ritter, at the age of 12, the song became a favorite among the British blues bands of the sixties. The Nashville Teens, believing that Loudermilk lightning could strike twice, also recorded John D.'s "Google Eye" and were rewarded with another British top ten record – after which they never made it again!

I Can't Stop Loving You

Another Hank Williams classic and one that Ray Charles recorded in 1962 as part of his "Modern Sounds In Country And Western" album project. Other Country-oriented hits resulting from these sessions include Hank's "Your Cheatin' Heart," Fred Rose's "Take These Chains From My Heart," Harlan Howard's "Busted" and Cindy Walker and Eddy Arnold's "You Don't Know Me." This accumulation of bestsellers resulted in Charles becoming the biggest name in American black music. Later, in 1983, with his recording career in the doldrums, Ray Charles signed a new recording contract, with CBS, and once more returned to Nashville to renew the Country connection.

Act Naturally

Penned by Von Morrison and Johnny Russell, this ditty about achieving success in show biz became a Country chart-topper for Buck Owens. Later it was recorded by The Beatles, with Ringo Starr handling the vocal, eventually becoming part of a double-sided hit (the other side being "Yesterday") in 1965. Ringo always had something of a penchant for Country sounds and soon after embarking on his solo career, he headed for Nashville in order to cut a Country album called "Beaucoup Of Blues." Paul McCartney also wasn't adverse to Country sounds and, during the seventies, flew down to Nashville, where he and his wife Linda recorded under the pseudonym "The Country Hams."

| *This Ole House* | Stuart Hamblen wrote this one after a hunting trip in Texas, during which he found the body of a dead trapper in a ramshackle hut miles from the nearest road. Hamblen, who penned the song on the back of an old sandwich bag, had a half-million seller with his own version of "This Ole House" but took a back-seat when Rosemary Clooney got into the act, her recording selling over two million copies in the USA alone during 1954. In 1981 Welsh rockabilly Shakin' Stevens revived the song once more and was rewarded when his version provided him with his first British chart-topper. |

| *Release Me* | Acclaimed as one of the most popular songs of the year in 1954, when Ray Price's original version was released, "Release Me," written by Eddie Miller and Dub Williams, was a massive success for R & B vocalist Esther Phillips in 1962, when her record label encouraged her to cut a number of tracks similar in vein to those that were proving so profitable for Ray Charles. But though Phillips' version stayed in the US bestsellers for fourteen weeks, it made little impact in Britain and it wasn't until 1967, when Engelbert Humperdinck's rendition soared to number one in the UK charts, that the British public really became familiar with one of the world's most performed songs. |

| *A Good Year For The Roses* | Jerry Chestnut first tried to break into the music business during the fifties but soon gave up. In 1968, he tried again, this time as a songwriter. Almost immediately he achieved success and in 1970 George Jones just missed topping the US Country charts with his version of Chestnut's "A Good Year For The Roses." Eleven years later, British rock star and Country music fan Elvis Costello, who had previously appeared on George Jones' "My Very Special Guests" album, took his band, The Attractions, to Nashville and recorded his own album with the aid of producer Billy Sherrill. Costello's rendition of "A Good Year For The Roses" proved to be the first single culled from the sessions and this climbed the British pop charts with some alacrity, providing Costello with his third UK top ten hit. Later the rock star released his version of Don Gibson's "Sweet Dreams" as a follow-up but this hardly nudged into the top fifty. |

John D. Loudermilk and his wife

Elvis Costello and The Attractions

REMEMBER ME

Country trademarks

Dolly Parton's wigs

"I started doing my hair like this when I was in high school," Dolly told her biographer, Allana Nash. "The style – teasin' and all – was just out then, and I enjoyed it. Then it got out of style, but I still liked it that'a way. And then when everything started changin', people got to sayin', 'You should change your hairstyle. That's out of style.' And I thought, 'Well, they noticed. So it may be a gimmick in addition to something I enjoy. I'll just keep it this way to see who will notice and stir up as much interest as I can.' And the more interest I stirred up, the higher I put it, and the more extreme I got." Dolly began wearing wigs for convenience and then because her own hair had become damaged from all the years of teasing.

The hobo persona of Boxcar Willie

For 16 years, Cecil Travis Martin was a small-time Country singer called Marty Martin, who performed in the style of his heroes, Jimmie Rodgers, Ernest Tubb, Hank Williams and Lefty Frizzell, in the honky tonks round his home near Dallas, Texas. But Martin dreamed of one day being a star, dressed in the guise of a railroad hobo, and even kept a suitable costume in a box under his bed. He never dared appear in public wearing it until a night in October 1975 when he was so disgusted by the CMA Awards, some of which went to pop artists like John Denver, that he resolved to do something about the demise of "real Country Music." He told his wife, "Honey, I'm gonna win a major Country Music award within five years," then pulled the box from under his bed – and so Boxcar Willie was born.

Jerry Lee Lewis' right leg

When Jerry Lee Lewis is in full cry during a performance his right leg is invariably sticking out straight, at an angle to the piano. This curious stance goes back to the formative years of his childhood when, at the age of 13, he broke his hip and thigh bone in a football game. His leg was in a cast for two months and he had to play the piano with it stretched out. It became a habit that he's never grown out of.

Roy Acuff's Yo-Yo

Roy took up yo-yoing in 1931, when he was still recuperating from the severe bout of sunstroke and nervous exhaustion that terminated his interest in a baseball career. Practically housebound, he spent many hours attempting trick "throws" with the yo-yo and became such an expert that he later decided to feature his dexterity with the toy as part of his stage act. In 1974, he even gave a Presidential yo-yo lesson during the ceremony that marked the opening of the new Nashville Opryhouse.

Minnie Pearl's price-tagged hat

Legend has it that Minnie was so excited by the prospect of her first stage appearance that she played the whole show before remembering that she hadn't removed the price tag from her new, wide-brimmed straw hat. Since then, she says, she's retained both the hat and the tag (or rather their descendants) as symbols of good luck. Whether or not she actually bought that first chapeau is open to speculation, for as long as most folk remember, Minnie has always made her own hats, wearing them for many, many years. Still, the one in the Country Music Hall of Fame, a model she wore at the time of her first Opry appearance, seems to be in pretty good shape.

Johnny Cash's black clothes

The very first public performance by Johnny Cash and the Tennessee Two (Luther Perkins and Marshall Grant) was at a church in North Memphis. "One of our neighbors who had heard us asked if we'd do a few songs in their Sunday night service," Cash explained in his book, *Man In Black*. "We had talked about clothes and thought we should try to dress alike, but nobody had a nice suit, and the only colored shirts we had alike were black. 'Black will be better for church anyway,' I said, so we wore black shirts and pants. To this day, when someone asks me why I wear black, I can never really think of a simple answer, so I often say 'Black is better for church.'"

Don Williams' hat

"The hat was given to me by the people at 20th Century Fox when I was making *W.W. And The Dixie Dancekings* with Burt Reynolds," says Don Williams. "I really had worn hats very little prior to that. But the guy who styled it for me, it was his specialty to style hats to a person's features, and I just, little by little, got into wearing it more and more until it became just like part of me. I kid about it turning into a growth, but I really don't feel right if I go outside without wearing it. I feel like I'm not dressed." Don now has several identical hats, all custom-made for him by a company in Missouri.

Johnny Cash, Man in Black

Don Williams with his hatmaker

SING HIGH, SING LOW

The Jordanaires list

The Jordanaires are probably the most recorded vocal group in the world. Formed in 1948 in Springfield, Missouri, they came to prominence in the USA by winning the Arthur Godfrey Talents Scout TV show in 1956 and found international fame when they backed Elvis Presley on his many RCA hit records. They've worked on dozens of TV shows, over 30 film soundtracks and literally thousands of records, mostly Country. Gordon Stoker, who's been a member of The Jordanaires almost from their beginnings, has put together this list of some of the artists that The Jordanaires have worked with on many occasions:

Hank Williams – and later Hank Williams Jr – Red Foley, Hank Snow, Tennessee Ernie Ford, Patsy Cline, Carl Perkins, Johnny Cash, Marty Robbins, Loretta Lynn, Webb Pierce, Rick Nelson, Tommy Sands, Peter and Gordon, Patti Page, Kitty Wells, Jim Reeves, Eddy Arnold, Faron Young, Connie Frances, Ferlin Huskey, Conway Twitty, Don Gibson, Johnny Rivers, Gene Pitney, Ringo Starr, Elvis Presley, Ray Price, Gene Vincent, George Jones, Tammy Wynette, Charley Pride, Tom Jones, B.J. Thomas, Kenny Rogers, Jerry Reed, Sonny James, Moe Bandy, Barbara Mandrell, Roy Clark, Don McLean, Merle Haggard, Ronnie Milsap, Perry Como, Tex Ritter, Dottie West, Boxcar Willie, Lynn Anderson, Gary Stewart, Lefty Frizzell, Ronnie McDowell, Floyd Cramer, Ray Stevens, Tanya Tucker, Chet Atkins, Glen Campbell (when he was a studio musician), Tom T. Hall, Charlie Daniels (when he was a studio musician), Dolly Parton, Sylvia, Waylon Jennings, Roy Orbison, Jerry Lee Lewis, Jimmy Dean (The Jordanaires played an important role on his hit record "Big Bad John"), Bill Anderson, Johnny Horton (including the huge hit "Battle Of New Orleans"), Pat Boone, Ann-Margret . . .

Elvis Presley with The Jordanaires

SING ME A SONG, MR RODEO MAN

Chris LeDoux's rodeo rides

Chris LeDoux is not only a fine singer and songwriter but also, in December 1976, became the winner of the world championship bareback riding title at the National Finals Rodeo, in Oklahoma City, the "superbowl" of rodeo. Here, Wyoming's Singing Cowboy lists some of his toughest rides.

Three Bars

She's a little mare that belongs to Reg Kesler and is probably one of the most ornery bareback horses of all time. She threw me off at the National Finals Rodeo in 1973 and I had her again at Houston in 1977. When I found out I'd drawn her in the final round I sure wasn't tickled – there were other horses I would much rather have got on. When the time came to ride, she turned out of the chute and went to bucking. The further she went, the stronger she got. And the further she went, the looser I got. Finally the whistle blew and my hand was jerked out of the rigging – at which point I landed on my head in the arena dirt. I must have made Three Bars mad 'cause when I looked up, I could see her mouth was open and her ears were laid back. If she'd only been in a position to get me I'm sure she'd have done a little stampin'. Yeah, she's one little mare with a heart bigger than her backside.

Devil's Partner

Back in '70, I was rodeo riding hard, trying to make it to my first National Finals. At one point I was in Gladewater, Texas, where we got two bareback horses. I placed on my first one and was a little concerned about which day I would get my second horse because I was entered at another rodeo in Beaumont, Texas, that same week. I remembered seeing a horse called Devil's Partner in the bareback riding at an earlier performance. He was an older horse who'd gained much fame over the years. Anyway, a cowboy named John Chambers was havin' a tough time in the chute with him. Ole Partner would rave and mash him to the back side, along with trying to bite him. And when he did turn out, Partner clunked him down pretty hard. But I remember thinking that I'd rather draw Devil's Partner than still be riding in Gladewater the same day I was supposed to be in Beaumont. Well, I guess the Lord must have heard that 'cause I drew up on the same day and did get Devil's Partner. Some of the guys told me how to handle the horse in the chute. They said the best way was to pull the riggin' real easy and not to sit on him until the gate was opened. If I did that, they said, he wouldn't mash me. So I did what they told me and it worked. He blew out of there and went to buckin'. After about three jumps, I really felt good and, man, *he* felt good. The further he went, the stronger he got. My head started poppin' with every jump and each jump I'd black out, my senses clearing to see his head and neck and enabling me to plant my spurs. Then my head would pop again and so things went until the whistle finally blew. Afterwards my neck felt like it was as big around as a basket ball. But I won the go-round and the rodeo and was mighty, mighty, happy.

Tee Pee Every Fourth of July I'd try to work Cody, Wyoming, Red Lodge, Montana and Livingstone, Montana, all on the same day. The various rodeo committees had their time schedules set so that riders could do this. Cody would start at one. Red Lodge, some sixty miles away, started at three, and Livingstone, one hundred and fifty miles from Red Lodge, began at eight. By the time we got to Livingstone I was pretty well played out – and sore! That year I drew a horse called Tee Pee. An average sort of a horse and not one to get nervous about – in fact, I can remember getting on him and joking with some of the guys before nodding my head for the gate. Anyway, he turned out of the chute and went jumping and kicking straight across the arena. So I really opened up on him and when I got too wild, he'd duck under my foot, leaving both my legs on one side. Then I'd get back in the middle of him and start spurring again – at which point he'd duck under my foot once more. Now this stiff was getting a little old and I wasn't going to win anything the way things were going, so I straighted around again and began spurring some more. Pretty quick we were right in front of the grandstands – which is where Tee Pee decided that he'd try to make a hole in the wall. He tried to do so by slamming into the boards and bouncing off, missing mashing my foot by just a whisker. But when he came off the wall, I opened up again – only to find that my spur was still hanging in the fence! All of a sudden, things began to happen – much faster than I could think. Tee Pee jerked me out parallel with his back while my spur was still hung in the fence and my hand in the rigging. Then my spur came loose and I was flung over the horse's back and down underneath him, where he proceeded to tramp a mud hole in me. Thankfully, I escaped with my life, though I felt pretty battered. As for ole Tee Pee, he merely trotted back to the catch pen, proud as proud can be!

SING ME BACK HOME

Favorite songs of the stars

We asked several Country performers to choose their favorite songs. Not surprisingly, several chose the songs that were responsible for launching their hit-making careers, including David Frizzell with "You're The Reason God Made Oklahoma," his first duet success with Shelly West; Porter Wagoner with "Satisfied Mind," his chart debut for RCA in 1955; and Johnny Lee with "Lookin' For Love," the theme song from the movie *Urban Cowboy* which made him a star.

Porter Wagoner's Favorite Songs

Satisfied Mind
Trouble In The Amen Corner
Just Someone I Used To Know
Blue Eyes Crying In The Rain
Great Speckled Bird
Ole Slew Foot
Don't Be Cruel
(Now And Then There's) A Fool Such As I
She Thinks I Still Care
I Will Always Love You

The Oak Ridge Boys' Favorite Songs

Joe Bonsall *Maria* (from *West Side Story*)
Duane Allen *McArthur Park*
William Lee Golden *Faded Love*
Richard Sterban *You Needed Me*

George Hamilton IV's Favorite Songs

Forever Young
Life's Railway To Heaven
Dirty Old Man
Streets Of London
The Dutchman
I Don't Think Much About Her Any More
England
Carolina On My Mind
Canadian Railroad Trilogy
Poncho And Lefty

Johnny Lee's Favorite Songs

Lookin' For Love
Love Look What You've Done To Me
Statue Of A Fool
You Made Me So Very Happy
Blue Monday
Would You Take Another Chance On Me
Lonely Wine
I'm Sorry

"I love the song 'Lookin' For Love' because it changed my life, but also because it's a really good song," says Johnny Lee. "Rock 'n' roll was my first love and 'Blue Monday' has always been a favorite, a great song by Fats Domino. 'Would You Take Another Chance On Me' is a great performance by Jerry Lee Lewis and 'Lonely Wine' is probably my favorite song by Mickey Gilley."

David Frizzell's Favorite Songs

I Love You A Thousand Ways
Georgia On My Mind
You're The Reason God Made Oklahoma
I'm Gonna Hire A Wino To Decorate Our Home
Please Come To Boston
Wish I Could Hurt That Way Again
Mom And Dad Waltz
Today I Started Loving You Again
Little Green Apples
Husbands And Wives

David Frizzell

George Jones' Favorite Records

Tammy Wynette *Take Me To Your World*
Tom T. Hall *Old Side Of Town*
Leon Payne *I Love You Because*
Hank Williams *You Win Again*
The Kendalls *Heaven's Just A Sin Away*
Lefty Frizzell *Always Late*
Emmylou Harris *Making Believe*
Bill Monroe *Blue Moon Of Kentucky*
Ray Price *Crazy Arms*
Wynn Stewart *Such A Pretty World*

Narvel Felt's Favorite Songs

Stranger On The Shore
Reconsider Me
Drift Away
Blue Suede Shoes
Fraulein
My Prayer
Away
Four Seasons Of Life
Foggy Misty Morning
How Great Thou Art

Tom T. Hall's Favorite Songs

Somewhere Over The Rainbow
Far Away Places
White Christmas
How Great Thou Art
Foggy Mountain Breakdown
The First Time I Ever Saw Your Face
Feelings
Amazing Grace
I Care
I Love

Vern Gosdin's Favorite Songs

He Stopped Loving Her Today
The Way I Am
Play Me
Just Give Me What You Think Is Fair
If You're Gonna Do Me Wrong (Do It Right)
Boulder To Birmingham

Rattlesnake Annie's Favorite Songs

Till The End
Loving Her Was Easy
Amazing Grace
Dream Of Me

Goodbye To A River
Comanche Tears
No Man's Land
Walking
She Never Spoke Spanish To Me
Old Five And Dimers
Funky Country Living
Family Bible
I'm So Lonesome I Could Cry
Hang Him Higher

Rattlesnake Annie

124

The Kendalls

The Kendalls' Favorite Songs

Almost Persuaded

Heaven's Just A Sin Away

You Needed Me

Hello Darlin'

Window Up Above

There Goes My Everything

If I Could Only Win Your Love

Pittsburgh Stealers

Already Blue

Amanda

Royce and Jeannie Kendall agreed on their favorite records, though Jeannie was particularly keen to choose songs by her two favorite female singers, Emmylou Harris and Anne Murray, with "If I Could Only Win Your Love" and "You Needed Me" respectively. "Heaven's Just A Sin Away" and "Pittsburgh Stealers" are The Kendalls' two biggest hit records to date.

125

Roy Acuff

Fred Rose

Wesley Rose

126

SO MANY TIMES

Acuff-Rose's most recorded songs

Roy Acuff and Fred Rose formed Acuff–Rose, a Nashville-based publishing company, in 1942. Today, the company, headed by CMA founder-member Wesley Rose, is one of the world's leading music publishing houses.

Tennessee Waltz	*You Win Again*
Your Cheatin' Heart	*When Will I Be Loved*
I Can't Stop Loving You	*Singing The Blues*
Release Me	*Cryin'*
There Goes My Everything	*Half As Much*
Then You Can Tell Me Goodbye	*I Can't Help It If I Fall In Love With You*
Jambalaya	*('Til) I Kissed You*
Last Date	*I'll Be A Legend In My Time*
Cold Cold Heart	*Only The Lonely*
Oh Lonesome Me	*Send Me The Pillow You Dream On*
Oh Pretty Woman	*A White Sport Coat*
I Love You Because	*Lonely Street*
Jealous Heart	*Blue Eyes Crying In The Rain*
Sweet Dreams	*Take These Chains From My Heart*

SOMETHING SPECIAL

The Mel Tillis list

Ten songs authored or co-authored by Mel Tillis that became important records for other artists:

I'm Tired	Webb Pierce (1959 – No.3)
I Ain't Never	Webb Pierce (1959 – No.2)
All The Time	Kitty Wells (1959 – No.18)
Emotions	Brenda Lee (1961 – No.7 in the pop charts)
Heart Over Mind	Ray Price (1961 – No.5)
Detroit City	Bobby Bare (1963 – No.6, also No.16 in the pop charts)
Burning Memories	Ray Price (1964 – No.2)
Snakes Crawl At Night	Charley Pride (1965 – no hit, but important in that it was Charley's first record for RCA)
Mental Revenge	Waylon Jennings (1967 – No.12)
Ruby, Don't Take Your Love To Town	Kenny Rogers and The First Edition (1969 – No.6 in the pop charts)

Also, the three questions Mel is most often asked and the three replies he most often uses:

1. *Do you really stutter?*
"Yes, I d-d-d-do."

2. *How did you begin stuttering?*
"Well, it happened right after I caught malaria when I was about three. I also had a friend by the name of Leroy English who stuttered and I honestly don't know whether I started stuttering from being around Leroy as much as from the malaria . . . I think it's a bit of both. My mother was busy with us kids and whatever, and when I'd call for her when I was down in bed, if she didn't answer or didn't come right in I guess I'd repeat it. 'M-M-Mother!' And it worked. So I thought that was the right way to talk."

3. *Why don't you stutter when you sing?*
"I think it's the beat, the rhythm and also the identity. When I'm in front of the microphone, I become Mel Tillis the singer – almost like another person – and that other person doesn't stutter. All people who stutter or stammer can sing. By that I mean they will not repeat themselves when they're singing. It's even used as therapy by some specialists."

: Mel Tillis

SOMETHING'S WRONG IN CALIFORNIA

Movies we'd like to see with Country casts

1 *The Thin Man* with Roy Clark

2 *Two For The Road* with Dolly Parton

3 *Whistle Down The Wind* with Boxcar Willie

4 *Where Eagles Dare* with Glenn Frey and Don Henley

5 *Life With Father* with Hank Williams, Jr

6 *Whiskey Galore* with George Jones

7 *Picnic At Hanging Rock* with Willie Nelson

8 *What's Up Doc?* with Dennis Locorriere and Ray Sawyer

9 *The Killer Is Loose* with Jerry Lee Lewis

10 *All The King's Men* with The Original Drifting Cowboys

11 *A Yank At Oxford* with Kris Kristofferson

12 *The Producers* with Billy Sherrill and Pete Drake

13 *Three Smart Girls* with The Mandrell Sisters

14 *The Joker Is Wild* with Jerry Clower

15 *Black Gold* with Charley Pride

16 *The First Lady* with Kitty Wells

17 *The Family Way* with June, Helen and Anita Carter

18 *Hatter's Castle* with Minnie Pearl

19 *The Day Of The Outlaw* with Waylon Jennings

20 *Pal Joey* with Joe Ely

Right: Roy Clark

Below: Charley Pride and Jerry Clower

A Special Award
to
Charley Pride
On the
Achievement of 500,000 Album Sales in the U.
and to
Mark his Services to Country Music in Great B

131

TAKE THIS JOB AND SHOVE IT

Previous occupations of Country stars

T.G. Sheppard

A pop singer in the early sixties, he was signed to Atlantic Records and given the name Brian Stacy. He opened shows for the likes of The Beach Boys and Jan and Dean but with little success, then sought steadier employment on the other side of the music business as Regional Promotional man for RCA in Memphis.

Boxcar Willie

"I've flown planes, I was a disc jockey, ran a bowling alley, I was a mechanic, farmed, dug ditches, sold magazines, worked for Sears in the electrical department, I've always had two or three jobs at once. I never went to Nashville and sat there and starved. I always had a day-job."

Billy Swan

Several jobs, including gate-guard at Elvis' mansion, Graceland, in Memphis, and janitor at CBS Records in Nashville (when he quit he gave his job to Kris Kristofferson).

Mickey Gilley

"I couldn't make enough money to support my family in Ferriday, Louisiana, so I came to Houston with my father-in-law and started laying sanitary sewers. I was an 'oiler', a grease monkey really." Two years later his cousin, Jerry Lee Lewis, sent him his first record, which inspired Mickey to try his hand at performing and recording.

Roy Clark

In his late teens, Roy boxed in the light heavyweight division in the Washington DC area. He won 15 straight bouts before trading his gloves for a guitar.

Joe Stampley

"I had a job at a paper mill for a while. People there said I was crazy to try and enter the music business. The foreman told me I should stick with a steady job. The mill shut down a few years ago and all the men were laid off."

Johnny Cash

After four years in the US Air Force, Johnny went to Memphis to try and break into the music business. To support himself he took a job selling second-hand electrical equipment. "I hated every minute," he recalled later. "Once in a while, down in the poorer sections of town, I'd sell a used washing machine."

Moe Bandy

Bronco-busting, until a series of broken bones administered by "big, bad bucking broncs and perpetually pompous ponies" turned him to the gentler profession of music making, where one of his first hits was "Bandy The Rodeo Clown."

Moe Bandy

Johnny Cash

133

TENNESSEE SATURDAY NIGHT

The Grand Ole Opry cast

The Grand Ole Opry, an institution that's almost as old as Country music itself, began broadcasting in late 1925 over radio station WSM in Nashville, Tennessee and has apparently never missed a Saturday night transmission in its long history. Originally called WSM Barn Dance, the program won its unusual name from an ad-lib made by George D. Hay, the self-styled "Solemn Old Judge," who was the announcer for many years. The show followed an hour of classical music and one evening Hay announced, "For the past hour we have been listening to music taken largely from Grand Opera, but from now on we will present the Grand Ole Opry." Today's large cast includes regulars like Roy Acuff who rarely miss a show, and well-known contemporary Country stars like Don Williams and Dolly Parton, who make only occasional visits. Several have been connected with the Opry for several decades, including Herman Crook of the Crook Brothers, who made his debut in 1925, while others are young and joined only recently, notably Ricky Skaggs and Riders In The Sky, whose debut came in 1982. The Grand Ole Opry is watched each week by an audience of some 4400 in the Grand Ole Opry House at Opryland and listened to by a huge radio audience tuned to WSM's Clear Channel Frequency – 650 AM.

Some of the cast list . . .

Roy Acuff	Skeeter Davis
Bill Anderson	Little Jimmy Dickens
Ernie Ashworth	Roy Drusky
Boxcar Willie	The Four Guys
Jim Ed Brown	The Fruit Jar Drinkers
Archie Campbell	Larry Gatlin and the Gatlin Brothers Band
The Carlisles	Don Gibson
Jerry Clower	Billy Grammer
John Conlee	Jack Greene
Wilma Lee Cooper	Tom T. Hall
The Crook Brothers	George Hamilton IV

David Houston
Jan Howard
Stonewall Jackson
Jim and Jesse
George Jones
Grandpa Jones
Hank Locklin
Lonzo and Oscar
Charlie Louvin
Loretta Lynn
Barbara Mandrell
Kirk McGhee
Ronnie Milsap
Bill Monroe
Jimmy "C" Newman
The Osborne Brothers
Dolly Parton
Minnie Pearl
Stu Phillips
Ray Pillow
Jeanne Pruett

Del Reeves
Riders In The Sky
Jeannie Seely
Jean Shepard
The Tennessee Travelers
Ricky Skaggs
Connie Smith
Hank Snow
The Stoney Mountain Cloggers
B.J. Thomas
Ernest Tubb
Justin Tubb
Porter Wagoner
Billy Walker
Charlie Walker
Dottie West
The Wilburn Brothers
Don Williams
The Vic Willis Trio
Del Wood

Right: Some of the earliest performers on the Opry

Below: Riders In The Sky

THAT'S WHY I LEFT THE MOUNTAINS

The twelve chapters of "The Phantom Empire"

The serial *The Phantom Empire* provided Gene Autry with his first starring role, in 1935. Autry portrays a cowboy who discovers Murania, a secret future world, at the bottom of a mineshaft. Eventually, after various exploits amid "Flash Gordon"-type sets, he escapes from Murania at the very moment the land is to be destroyed by a giant deathray, and rides home to Radio Ranch, where he croons "Silver-Haired Daddy Of Mine" before the final credits roll.

1	*The Singing Cowboy*	7	*Jaws Of Jeopardy*
2	*The Thunder Riders*	8	*From Death To Life*
3	*The Lightning Chamber*	9	*Prisoners Of The Ray*
4	*The Phantom Broadcast*	10	*The Rebellion*
5	*Beneath The Earth*	11	*A Queen In Chains*
6	*Disaster From The Skies*	12	*End Of Murania*

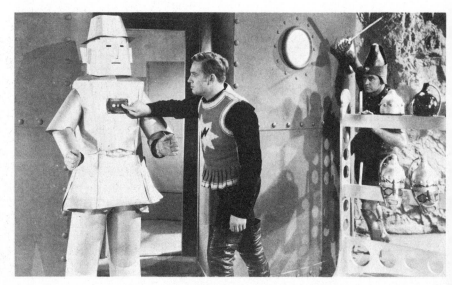

Gene Autry with robotic friend

TIME CHANGES EVERYTHING

Country stars as they looked yesterday – and today

The Oak Ridge Boys

Today, the Oak Ridge Boys are Country-pop superstars but originally they were a popular gospel group, the Oak Ridge Quartet. In between these two periods they were known simply as The Oaks. The vintage photograph comes from a TV taping for the Mike Douglas Show in October 1973. Ten years on, their look, and style of clothes, has changed dramatically, but they still adopt the same left-to-right line-up on stage: Joe Bonsall, Duane Allen, Bill Golden and Richard Sterban.

The Oak Ridge Boys:
Joe, Duane, Bill, Richard
Top: yesterday *Below:* today

Mel Tillis

Mel's fame has grown with his hair. The first picture comes from the days when he was signed to Decca and was only moderately well known as a singer, but had scored considerable success as a songwriter, with hits like "Detroit City."

Mel Tillis yesterday

Mel Tillis today

Tanya Tucker

Tanya Tucker, the innocent-looking teenager from 1972, when she scored a controversial country chart-topper with David Allan Coe's "Would You Lay With Me In A Field Of Stone," is now a sophisticated young woman.

Tanya Tucker yesterday

Tanya Tucker today

Hank Williams Jr

Hank is pictured here as a teenager in the sixties, and as he looks twenty years on. His beard covers some of the scars from injuries he suffered after a near fatal fall in the Montana Rockies in August 1975. Plastic surgery and recuperative treatment lasted for a period of two years.

Hank Williams Jr yesterday

Hank Williams Jr today

Gene Watson

Few singers have changed their appearance so dramatically as Gene Watson, the former body-shop mechanic from Texas. Though his looks have changed, his music hasn't: he's still scoring hits with his strong, pure Country style.

Gene Watson yesterday

Gene Watson today

Tompall and The Glaser Brothers

The clean-shaven Glaser Brothers look stems from the first phase of their career as a popular Country trio, which began when they came to Nashville in 1957 and continued until they split up in 1973; and the hairy style comes after their reunion at the 1979 Wembley Country Festival in England.

Tompall and The Glaser Brothers
Top: yesterday   *Below:* today

Jimmy "C" Newman

The photo of the young Mr Newman comes from his period with Decca Records when he had still to add the "C" (for "Cajun") to his name. Jimmy has recently built a very strong following for his engaging brand of Cajun-flavored Country music in Europe.

Jimmy "C" Newman
Top: yesterday   *Below:* today

TOE TAPPIN' MUSIC

The Burritos list Country-rock bands

The Burritos – Gib Guilbeau and John Beland – provide their views on other bands that have figured in Country-rock history.

The Eagles

They're friends of ours. When we left Linda Ronstadt, The Eagles became our replacement band. We played with Glen Frey and some of the others way back and we knew, even then, that they would do something great with themselves because they were so unbelievably talented. Frey and Henley are like the Lennon and McCartney of Country-rock.

Poco

A very good band who were coming up with great harmonies even before The Eagles. They never got the proper credit due to them and it's unfortunate that The Eagles overshadowed them as much as they did.

The Nitty Gritty Dirt Band

The Dirt Band were very instrumental in tying the young in with Nashville. They came to Nashville with their long hair but still managed to make friends with conservative people like Roy Acuff and, subsequently, did much for both rock and Country. We used to go down and see The Nitty Gritty Dirt Band, at The Troubadour during the sixties. If you ever wanted a good time, they were the band to see.

The Dillards

We have always loved 'em. Another underrated group with great harmonies. They should be given credit for doing many of the things years ago that Ricky Skaggs is doing right now. If there was some sort of Hall of Fame for Country-rock then The Dillards would be the first to get elected. Rodney Dillard is a genius at what he does and probably the best Dillards line-up was the one that included Rodney, Mitch Jayne, Dean Webb and Herb Pederson.

Country Gazette

They're sorta like The Dillards in a way but more traditional, more into bluegrass. As pickers they've always been excellent and should rate right up there alongside such people as Bill Monroe in the bluegrass field. They've always managed to retain their own crowd and, unlike The Dirt Band, they've never felt the need to change.

Pure Prairie League

Just an average Country-rock outfit really. They never really made it because they were basically just a weak imitation of what was going on in Los Angeles at the time.

Mike Nesmith's Various Bands

Mike, he was always very talented, pretty smart – which is why he's involved in one of America's top video companies these days. But even back in the sixties he was instrumental in getting The Monkees to do a lot of Country things.

Rick Nelson's Stone Canyon Band

Rick was another who never got the credit for many of the things he did. He was pre-Poco, pre most things. He was the first performer to come out in L.A. with a pedal steel-man and he had people like Randy Meisner and Tom Brumley playing with him. In our eyes he was a true pioneer.

Gib Guilbeau (*left*) and John Beland – The Burritos

Lloyd Green

TULSA TIME

Benelux Country favorites

Country Gazette is the leading Country publication in Holland and Belgium and these are the results of its most recent annual polls:

1981

Male Vocalist	**1** Don Williams, **2** Merle Haggard, **3** Johnny Cash
Female Vocalist	**1** Emmylou Harris, **2** Dolly Parton, **3** Tammy Wynette
Group	**1** Statler Brothers, **2** Oak Ridge Boys, **3** Tompall and the Glaser Brothers
Duo	**1** George Jones and Tammy Wynette, **2** Porter Wagoner and Dolly Parton, **3** Bellamy Brothers
Songwriter	**1** Don Williams, **2** Merle Haggard, **3** Kris Kristofferson
Instrumentalist	**1** Lloyd Green, **2** Chet Atkins, **3** Buddy Emmons
Bluegrass Group	**1** Country Gentlemen, **2** Bluegrass Cardinals, **3** Jim and Jesse and the Virginia Boys
Country/Bluegrass Group (national)	**1** Tulsa, **2** Cool Breeze, **3** Jerrycan
Country/Bluegrass Vocalist (national)	**1** Ruud Hermans (singer with Tulsa), **2** Ben Steneker, **3** Joni de Boer (singer with Tulsa)

1982

Male Vocalist	**1** Don Williams, **2** Merle Haggard, **3** Johnny Cash
Female Vocalist	**1** Emmylou Harris, **2** Dolly Parton, **3** Loretta Lynn
Group	**1** Tompall and the Glaser Brothers, **2** Alabama, **3** Statler Brothers
Duo	**1** Waylon and Willie, **2** Merle Haggard and George Jones, **3** David Frizzell and Shelly West
Songwriter	**1** Don Williams, **2** Merle Haggard, **3** Bob McDill
Instrumentalist	**1** Lloyd Green, **2** Ricky Skaggs, **3** Chet Atkins
Bluegrass Group	**1** Bluegrass Cardinals, **2** Country Gentlemen, **3** Joe Val and the New England Bluegrass Boys
Country/Bluegrass Group (national)	**1** Tulsa, **2** Groundspeed, **3** Canyon Drive Band
Country/Bluegrass Vocalist (national)	**1** Ruud Hermans, **2** Joni de Boer, **3** Ben Steneker

TURN YOUR RADIO ON

Country Music radio stations in North America

This list, which is based on an annual survey by the Country Music Association, shows how Country music radio has boomed in North America, particularly since 1978. "Country music radio airplay has made a great difference in the growth of the industry," said CMA Executive Director Jo Walker-Meador, after the publication of the 1983 survey. "This has been apparent over the last five years with so many stations switching to a Country format, the result being that Country music now stands second only to rock in radio listenership and record sales."

Number of full-time Country radio stations in the USA and Canada 1961–1983

Year	Stations	Year	Stations
1961	81	**1975**	1116
1963	97	**1977**	1140
1965	208	**1978**	1150
1969	606	**1979**	1434
1971	525	**1980**	1534
1972	633	**1981**	1785
1973	764	**1982**	2133
1974	856	**1983**	2266

Bobby Helms (*center*) at an informal broadcast

VOLKSWAGEN

West German Country favorites

The leading West German Country music publication, *Country Gazette*, has held a readers' poll on three occasions:

1979

Male Vocalist	**1** Johnny Cash, **2** Waylon Jennings, **3** Don Williams
Female Vocalist	**1** Emmylou Harris, **2** Dolly Parton, **3** Tammy Wynette
Instrumentalist	**1** Charlie McCoy, **2** Chet Atkins, **3** Floyd Cramer
Songwriter	**1** Kris Kristofferson, **2** Tom T. Hall, **3** Johnny Cash
Bluegrass	**1** Bill Monroe, **2** Flatt and Scruggs, **3** Jim and Jesse

1982

Male Vocalist	**1** Johnny Cash, **2** Bobby Bare, **3** Waylon Jennings
Female Vocalist	**1** Emmylou Harris, **2** Lacy J. Dalton and Dolly Parton
Group/Duo	**1** Statler Brothers, **2** Oak Ridge Boys, **3** Alabama
Instrumentalist	**1** Chet Atkins, **2** Charlie McCoy, **3** Lloyd Green
Songwriter	**1** Kris Kristofferson, **2** Tom T. Hall, **3** Johnny Cash
Bluegrass	**1** Bill Monroe, **2** Osborne Brothers, **3** Jim and Jesse
Vocalist (national)	**1** Gunter Gabriel, **2** Freddy Quinn, **3** Tom Astor
Group (national)	**1** Truck Stop, **2** Emsland Hillbillies, **3** Kentucky Bluefield

1983

Male Vocalist	**1** Johnny Cash, **2** Don Williams, **3** Merle Haggard
Female Vocalist	**1** Emmylou Harris, **2** Dolly Parton, **3** Loretta Lynn
Group/Duo	**1** Statler Brothers, **2** Alabama, **3** Oak Ridge Boys
Instrumentalist	**1** Chet Atkins, **2** Charlie McCoy, **3** Roy Clark
Songwriter	**1** Kris Kristofferson, **2** Bob McDill, **3** Tom T. Hall
Bluegrass	**1** Bill Monroe, **2** Osborne Brothers, **3** Jim and Jesse
Newcomer	**1** Ricky Skaggs, **2** Sylvia, **3** George Strait
Vocalist (national)	**1** Tom Astor, **2** Freddy Quinn, **3** Gunter Gabriel
Group (national)	**1** Truck Stop, **2** Western Union, **3** Emsland Hillbillies

Truck Stop

WE'RE NUMBER ONE

The Gatlins' all-time favorite harmony singing groups

1   Larry Gatlin and The Gatlin Brothers Band
2   The Blackwood Brothers
3   The Statesmen
4   The Imperials
5   The Anita Kerr Singers
6   The Mills Brothers
7   The Sons of the Pioneers
8   Norman Luboff Choir
9   The Statler Brothers
10   Tompall and The Glaser Brothers

Rudy was two, Steve three and Larry six when the Gatlin Brothers from Odessa, Texas, began singing together. "It really started with Larry," recalls Rudy. "He was the oldest and could talk and all that. One day my aunt said, 'Hey, why don't you have the other boys join in?' So we did." They found the first opportunity to sing together in public at church, and later began making the rounds of talent shows with their mother accompanying them on piano. They recorded their first album while still in their teens (for a small gospel label), then were split up when Larry went to college, though sang together whenever they were reunited. They cut a few singles together in 1972, but it wasn't until four years later and the album "Larry Gatlin, Family And Friends," which included the Grammy Award-winning hit "Broken Lady," that they really came to the fore. They're now recognized as one of the finest harmony singing groups in the world and have a unique style. "I'm not sure why our stuff doesn't sound like other people's," says Larry. "Our taste in music was shaped by various kinds of musical influences. We had an uncle who played piano. He was a great piano player and he liked jazz. He'd sit down and play an Ella Fitzgerald record or an Oscar Peterson. Of course, we started in gospel music – we liked the Blackwood Brothers and the Statesmen Quartet with Hove Lister, the old Southern-style gospel groups – but we were exposed at an early age to the musical hodgepodge in Texas, and we listen to everything from Country to jazz to classical. But we've always had our own sound, and we're grateful for that."

Larry Gatlin (*center*) and his brothers

WHATEVER HAPPENED TO RANDOLPH SCOTT?

The Statler Brothers list top entertainers

The Statler Brothers are among the best-loved and most respected acts in Country music. They've won over 300 awards, including three Grammy Awards, eight Country Music Association Awards and sixteen *Music City News* Awards. Noted for their patented harmonies, good humor and a keen lyrical sense (author Kurt Vonnegut once dubbed them "America's Poets"), The Statlers maintained the same line-up for nearly two decades until 1982, when Lew DeWitt retired and was replaced by young Jimmy Fortune. They all grew up in the same town – Staunton, Virginia – and began singing together as a group at the Lyndhurst Methodist Church. Staunton is still their home town and they have bought their old grade school and converted it into the Statler Brothers office. As they're one of the most entertaining groups in Country music we asked them for their own favorite entertainers.

Harold Reid   "I lean towards comedy for my favorite entertainment, and for me perhaps the funniest man in the world is Jonathan Winters. He entertains me from the moment he walks on stage. He may not be doing anything but he makes me laugh because I know that he's thinking about something funny."

Don Reid   "The comedian that I most admire in terms of being able to handle himself is Steve Allen. He's the most in-command performer that I've ever watched."

Phil Balsey   "I'd go for some of the great gospel quartets that have entertained me over the years; the Blackwood Brothers, The Statesmen, The Harvesters, who are no longer in existence, and the Rangers Quartet. I saw them a lot in my younger days and they always entertained me terrifically."

Jimmy Fortune "Don and Harold are two of the best performers that I've ever seen. I'd been a fan of the Statler Brothers for years and still have occasions when I can't believe that I'm in the same group as them! One of my favorite vocal groups was The Eagles. I really wish they were still together, but sadly they're not."

Harold, Jimmy, Don and Phil – The Statler Brothers

WHERE HAVE ALL OUR HEROES GONE?

Inspirations and influences

Willie Nelson

"I guess that I was greatly influenced by Floyd Tillman, Leon Payne, Tommy Duncan and, of course, Bob Wills. . . . There are a lot of guitar players that I have liked. Musicians like Hank 'Sugarfoot' Garland, George Barnes and Eldon Shamblin. Possibly Django Reinhardt was the daddy of them all. I guess that I am more of a Django Reinhardt fan than anybody else as far as guitar playing goes."

Joe Ely

"Bob Wills, Django Reinhardt and Stephane Grappelli were my inspirations. I think I went for Wills because he had something that was so much his own style, something completely apart from Nashville. I believe it's only now that people are beginning to realize what he actually did."

Jerry Naylor

"Johnny Horton was always a hero – and not only because he gave me my first job. Then too I'm a huge Bob Wills fan. Always was and most likely always will be. Then, along with a few other people, I particularly admire the sound of Ray Price, especially in his Cherokee Cowboys days. During the mid-seventies I cut a track called 'I Let Her Cry Me Back Again,' on which we got together as many of the original Cherokee Cowboys as we could possibly get. The song was written by Ray Pennington, who wrote several of Ray Price's hits, and it was great fun working on that session."

Charlie Daniels

"When I was playing bluegrass I was influenced by Bill Monroe, Lester Flatt and Earl Scruggs – just any good kind of bluegrass inspired me. I got into rock 'n' roll in the late fifties and really used to like Presley. Though if I had to name one idol, whose singing and writing I enjoyed, I'd have to say Willie Nelson."

Slim Whitman

"Jimmie Rodgers and a fella who called himself Montana Slim influenced me. Montana Slim came from out of Canada and his real name was Wilf Carter. At one time he had a network program out of New York and he came on with a 'yippy yeah and a heigh-ho' – or something like that. His style attracted me and I've since recorded several of his songs. Jimmie Rodgers – I grew up with his music. When I was a young fellow I would listen to Jimmie Rodgers records and say: 'I can do that yodel thing.' And I could. As a boy I could yodel – I think it's something you're actually born with."

Ed Bruce

"Many of my heroes were music or sports oriented. There was Johnny Cash, Carl Perkins and Chuck Berry. I never met the man but I'm still a great admirer of Willy Targell, who just retired after being with the Pittsburgh Pirates. Aside from being a great ballplayer he is a very articulate spokesman and a great humanitarian. I think one of the greatest heroes of recent years was Anwar Sadat. Harry Truman was a hero and Willie Nelson's a hero."

Waylon Jennings

"Muhammad Ali is my hero. He really is. I think he's the greatest thing to happen in twenty years." (Jennings talking to *Country Music* magazine in 1979.)

Terri Gibbs

"I learned harmonies from Everly Brothers and Patti Page records, rock from Elvis Presley and ballads from Pat Boone. And Ray Charles taught me soul."

Emmylou Harris

"I talk about George Jones too much, people think I'm a nut. But he's the greatest Country singer. There are some great old George Jones recordings that are just real funky stuff. The lyrics are great and he sings the hell out of them as well. Now he's mellowed out and he's doing stuff which is more crossover, I suppose."

George Jones

"When I was a kid, Roy Acuff was a big influence on me. I tried so hard to copy him at times, especially on my early Starday material. He's one of the greatest. Well, he is to me anyway. Likewise Ernest Tubb who I admire a lot."

Stella Parton

"Jimmie Rodgers – I sing his music all the time and use his style of guitar playing. I go down to the Jimmie Rodgers Memorial Festival in Meridian, Mississippi every year and one year they presented me with a lifetime membership award. They were showing a bit of his movie and I had to go and watch it every night that I was there – I've seen it over and over again."

George Jones

Emmylou Harris

WHY ME?

The worst gigs we ever played

Rosanne Cash

"I was in Munich on a promotional tour when I was told: 'We've got this gig, it's two hours out of Munich, you're gonna be playing to four thousand people and it's gonna be broadcast over Radio Luxembourg to six million listeners all over Europe.' We drove to this place called Heilbronn and the whole thing was supposed to be in a circus tent at noon. There were giraffes and tigers and all kinds of animals around this tent. I looked in and there were about eighty people there – then I discovered I had to walk into the centre ring and merely lip-synch in front of those people, while the show went out on the radio. I was so humiliated, walking out there in front of all those animals and things. But I did it. And all eighty people came down for my autograph when the show was over."

Rodney Dillard

"The Dillards once worked with a chimp act that went on before us – that's where we learned that you can't follow animal acts at State Fairs. There was this particular act, with all the chimps dressed up and the people going 'Ahhhhh . . .' outfront while the guy backstage yelled and screamed at them. The act began with a chimp riding out on a motorcycle. He'd motor onstage and a guy would put up his hand and stop him, like . . .zmmm–p! But after a week of this, one chimp got fed up with having all the crap beat out of him. He waited till Johnny Desmond had sung his song, with the help of an all-dressed-up orchestra in the pit. Then he went out dead on cue, roaring away in his best Evel Knievel style. He went right up to the guy onstage but this time didn't stop. He just rode right round him and shot straight off into the orchestra pit. Next minute there were violins flying, tuxedo tails, monkeys, bits of motorcycle – it was like something out of a cartoon. And we had to go on after that . . .!"

Janie Fricke

"One of my saddest jobs involved working for Elvis Presley. He'd recorded a TV show live in Rapid City and he and his back-up singers had already done some voice tracks. But I and a couple of other girls were asked to add our voices to those already done. Naturally we were all pretty excited and I remember thinking that Elvis might come in and surprise us while we were working. But then he died and we had to go in and finish the project after his death – which proved very hard on all of us. I'd felt so close to him because I'd lived in Memphis and because I was such a fan. But it was even worse for one of the other girls, who'd sung with him on such hits as 'Kentucky Rain' and 'Suspicious Minds'."

Johnny Lee

"I was playing at a rodeo at Gilley's in Pasadena, where they wanted me to make my grand entrance on a horse – but it was the biggest horse I'd ever seen in my life. I got on and the horse took a leap through the gate – and for every leap my pants ripped three inches. By the time we reached the middle of the arena, my pants were being held on by a snap at the front and a belt loop at the back. And I didn't have anything on underneath! I was supposed to dismount but all the spotlights were going to be turned on me and me alone – which meant that I was going to moon to about five thousand people. Not surprisingly, I was too embarrassed to get off and had the microphone thrown up to me. But then the horse got spooked and started bucking, at which point I threw the mike down and jumped off real quick, running to the safety of the bandstand, where I did the rest of the show from behind the drum kit."

Willie Nelson

"There was this place called The Country Dump," recalls Paul English, drummer with the Willie Nelson Band, remembering a Fort Worth club where the band played during the fifties. "They hired us to cover up the noise of this big dice game they were runnin' in the back room. We were paid twenty-four dollars a week, playin' six nights. We played there for nine months and saw two killings and at least one good fight every night."

Dolly Parton

"When I was working with the Porter Wagoner Show a few years ago and was wearing the wigs, there was a little dancin' fiddle-player who was all over the stage – and he got his bow caught in my hair . . . which set that wig back about five years! Another time I went onstage with my shoes on the wrong feet, though the most embarrassing thing that ever happened to me was when I entered a Dolly Parton look-alike contest – and lost."

Rosanne Cash

Janie Fricke

Ronnie Prophet

Jeanne Pruett

Ronnie Prophet

"I remember one financially disastrous gig we did up in New Brunswick in 1982. The show wasn't publicized or given promotion in any way and though we ended up with a pretty good house considering what the promoter had done – we had about half a house in a small night club – I ended up with hardly enough money to pay the band. When it came down to that almighty dollar, I felt like killing the show's buyer. But we tried to be really nice about it and just packed our things and got out of town. Such situations come and go. Another guy paid me with a bad cheque a couple of years ago. It took me a year and a half to collect – but I did it."

Jeanne Pruett

"One time we did a show in South Dakota, when along came a windstorm that not only blew the microphones off-stage but also blew all the speakers over. But the fans were wonderful, they just stayed there in a crowd, all huddled together, and that's how they stayed till the wind died away. Then we re-set the stage, re-set the microphones and carried right on with the concert. I guess it's all to do with that old saying, 'the show must go on'. And shows must go on if fans wait things out as they did that day."

Margo Smith

(After playing a Wembley Festival date at which she tripped over a step and also encountered difficulties working with a hastily rehearsed pick-up band) "I remember particularly one show in Taylorville, Illinois, where I opened my mouth to sing and had a moth fly straight in. I guess that was something of a disaster. Tonight was another one. We made so many mistakes – it's so hard when you're not working with your own band."

WILD IN THE COUNTRY

The Country records of Elvis

Elvis Presley was always a country boy at heart. In 1943 he won a prize for singing Red Foley's "Old Shep" at a State Fair. On his first recording session for Sun, 1954, he recorded Bill Monroe's "Blue Moon Of Kentucky" and "I Love You Because," the Leon Payne song that became such a massive success for Jim Reeves. Here's a list of some other Country songs that Elvis recorded, together with a tally of those with whom the songs are associated Countrywise.

Below: Johnny Cash with Elvis Presley

Hank Snow	*A Fool Such As I*
Darrell Glenn	*Crying In The Chapel*
Joe South	*Walk A Mile In My Shoes*
Bob Wills	*Faded Love*
Mickey Newbury	*American Trilogy*
Jerry Reed	*Big Boss Man*
Porter Wagoner	*Green Green Grass Of Home*
Marty Robbins	*You Gave Me A Mountain*
Jim Reeves	*Welcome To My World*
Ray Price	*Release Me*
Jack Greene	*There Goes My Everything*
Eddy Arnold	*You Don't Know Me*
Hank Williams	*I'm So Lonesome I Could Cry*
Anne Murray	*Snowbird*
Ned Miller	*From A Jack To A King*
Bill Monroe	*Little Cabin On The Hill*
Carl Perkins	*Blue Suede Shoes*
Jerry Reed	*US Male*
Ray Price	*For The Good Times*
Hank Williams	*Your Cheatin' Heart*
Kris Kristofferson	*Why Me Lord*
Billy Swan	*I Can Help*

Willie Nelson	*Funny How Time Slips Away*
Jerry Reed	*Guitar Man*
Jim Reeves	*He'll Have To Go*
Kris Kristofferson	*Help Me Make It Through The Night*
Bill Monroe	*Uncle Pen*
Tex Ritter	*Have I Told You Lately That I Love You*
Larry Gatlin	*Bitter They Are*

THE WINNER

The Music City News Award Winners

The Music City News Awards show, held each June at the start of Fan Fair week in Nashville, is the most important fan-voted awards presentation, and the only one to be broadcast live on network television. *Music City News*, a monthly magazine, is the longest-running Country music publication in America and was started by the singer Faron Young. "The reason we started *Music City News*," he explained later, "was because we didn't have a trade journal in the Country music industry. There were all those screen magazines and rock 'n' roll magazines, but Country music had nothing." The Music City News Awards were first sponsored in 1966 and the results reflect the particular favorites of America's Country music fans – Marty Robbins, The Statler Brothers, Barbara Mandrell, The Osborne Brothers, Conway Twitty, Loretta Lynn and Tompall and The Glaser Brothers.

1967

Male Artist	Merle Haggard
Female Artist	Loretta Lynn
Most Promising Male Artist	Tom T. Hall
Most Promising Female Artist	Tammy Wynette
Songwriter	Bill Anderson
Song Of The Year	"There Goes My Everything" (writer: Dallas Frazier)
Band	The Buckaroos
Vocal Group	Tompall and The Glaser Brothers
Duet	The Wilburn Brothers

1968

Male Artist	Merle Haggard
Female Artist	Loretta Lynn
Most Promising Male Artist	Cal Smith
Most Promising Female Artist	Dolly Parton
Songwriter	Bill Anderson
Band	The Buckaroos
Vocal Group	Tompall and The Glaser Brothers
Duet	Porter Wagoner and Dolly Parton

1969

Male Artist	Charley Pride
Female Artist	Loretta Lynn
Most Promising Male Artist	Johnny Bush
Most Promising Female Artist	Peggy Sue
Songwriter	Bill Anderson
Song Of The Year	"All I Have To Offer You Is Me" (writers: Dallas Frazier and Doodle Owens)
Band	The Buckaroos
Vocal Group	Tompall and The Glaser Brothers
Duet	Porter Wagoner and Dolly Parton
Instrumentalist	Roy Clark
Country TV Show	Tie: "Hee Haw" and "Johnny Cash Show"

1970

Male Artist	Charley Pride
Female Artist	Loretta Lynn
Most Promising Male Artist	Tommy Cash
Most Promising Female Artist	Susan Raye
Songwriter	Merle Haggard
Song Of The Year	"Hello Darlin'" (writer: Conway Twitty)
Band	The Buckaroos
Vocal Groups	Tompall and The Glaser Brothers
Duet	Porter Wagoner and Dolly Parton
Instrumentalist	Roy Clark
Country TV Show	"Hee Haw"

1971

Male Artist	Charley Pride
Female Artist	Loretta Lynn
Most Promising Male Artist	Tommy Overstreet
Most Promising Female Artist	Susan Raye
Songwriter	Kris Kristofferson
Song Of The Year	"Help Me Make It Through The Night" (writer: Kris Kristofferson)
Band	The Strangers
Vocal Group	The Statler Brothers
Duet	Conway Twitty and Loretta Lynn
Instrumentalist	Roy Clark
Comedy Act	Mel Tillis
Bluegrass Group	The Osborne Brothers
Country TV Show	"Hee Haw"

1972

Male Artist	Charley Pride
Female Artist	Loretta Lynn
Most Promising Male Artist	Billy "Crash" Craddock
Most Promising Female Artist	Donna Fargo
Songwriter	Kris Kristofferson
Song Of The Year	"Kiss An Angel" (writer: Ben Peters)
Band	The Strangers
Vocal Group	The Statler Brothers
Duet	Conway Twitty and Loretta Lynn
Instrumentalist	Roy Clark
Comedy Act	Archie Campbell
Bluegrass Group	The Osborne Brothers
Country TV Show	"Hee Haw"

1973

Male Artist	Charley Pride
Female Artist	Loretta Lynn
Most Promising Male Artist	Johnny Rodriguez
Most Promising Female Artist	Tanya Tucker
Songwriter	Kris Kristofferson
Song Of The Year	"Why Me" (writer: Kris Kristofferson)
Band	The Po' Boys
Vocal Group	The Statler Brothers
Duet	Conway Twitty and Loretta Lynn
Instrumentalist	Charlie McCoy
Comedy Act	Mel Tillis
Bluegrass Group	The Osborne Brothers
Country TV Show	"Hee Haw"

1974

Male Artist	Conway Twitty
Female Artist	Loretta Lynn
Most Promising Male Artist	Johnny Rodriguez
Most Promising Female Artist	Olivia Newton-John
Songwriter	Bill Anderson
Song Of The Year	"You've Never Been This Far Before" (writer: Conway Twitty)
Band	The Buckaroos
Vocal Group	The Statler Brothers
Duet	Conway Twitty and Loretta Lynn

Instrumentalist	Roy Clark
Instrumental Entertainer	Charlie McCoy
Comedy Act	Mel Tillis
Bluegrass Group	The Osborne Brothers
Country TV Show	"Hee Haw"
Touring Road Show	Loretta Lynn/Coalminers/Kenny Starr

1975

Male Artist	Conway Twitty
Female Artist	Loretta Lynn
Most Promising Male Artist	Ronnie Milsap
Most Promising Female Artist	Crystal Gayle
Songwriter	Bill Anderson
Song Of The Year	"Country Bumpkin" (writer: Don Wayne)
Band	The Coalminers
Vocal Group	The Statler Brothers
Duet	Conway Twitty and Loretta Lynn
Instrumentalist	Buck Trent
Instrumental Entertainer	Roy Clark
Comedy Act	Mel Tillis
Bluegrass Group	The Osborne Brothers
Country TV Show	"Hee Haw"

Loretta Lynn

Mickey Gilley

1976

Male Artist	Conway Twitty
Female Artist	Loretta Lynn
Most Promising Male Artist	Mickey Gilley
Most Promising Female Artist	Barbara Mandrell
Songwriter	Bill Anderson
Song Of The Year	"Blue Eyes Crying In The Rain" (writer: Fred Rose)
Band	The Coalminers
Vocal Group	The Statler Brothers
Duet	Conway Twitty and Loretta Lynn
Instrumentalist	Buck Trent
Instrumental Entertainer	Roy Clark
Comedy Act	Mel Tillis
Bluegrass Group	The Osborne Brothers
Country TV Show	"Hee Haw"
Album	"When A Tingle Becomes A Chill" (Loretta Lynn)
Founders' Award	Faron Young

1977

Male Artist	Conway Twitty
Female Artist	Loretta Lynn
Most Promising Male Artist	Larry Gatlin
Most Promising Female Artist	Helen Cornelius
Songwriter	Larry Gatlin
Song Of The Year	"I Don't Want To Have To Marry You" (writers: Fred Imus and Phil Sweet)
Band	The Coalminers
Vocal Group	The Statler Brothers
Duet	Conway Twitty and Loretta Lynn
Instrumentalist	Johnny Gimble
Instrumental Entertainer	Roy Clark
Comedy Act	Mel Tillis
Bluegrass Group	The Osborne Brothers
Country TV Show	"Hee Haw"
Album	"I Don't Want To Have To Marry You" (Jim Ed Brown and Helen Cornelius)
Founders' Award	Ralph Emery

Eddie Rabbitt

Marty Robbins

1978

Male Artist	Larry Gatlin
Female Artist	Loretta Lynn
Most Promising Male Artist	Don Williams
Most Promising Female Artist	Debby Boone
Songwriter	Larry Gatlin
Single	"Heaven's Just A Sin Away" (The Kendalls, artist; Jerry Gillespie, writer)
Bluegrass Group	The Osborne Brothers
Instrumentalist	Roy Clark
Comedy Act	Mel Tillis
Vocal Group	The Statler Brothers
Album	"Moody Blue" (Elvis Presley)
Duet	Conway Twitty and Loretta Lynn
Band	Larry Gatlin, Family and Friends
Country TV Show	"50 Years Of Country Music"
Founders' Award	Ernest Tubb

1979

Male Artist	Kenny Rogers
Female Artist	Barbara Mandrell
Most Promising Male Artist	Rex Allen, Jr
Most Promising Female Artist	Janie Fricke
Songwriter	Eddie Rabbitt
Single	"The Gambler" (Kenny Rogers, artist; Don Schlitz, writer)
Bluegrass Group	The Osborne Brothers

164

Musician	Roy Clark
Comedy Act	Jerry Clower
Vocal Group	The Statler Brothers
Album	"Entertainers On And Off The Road" (The Statler Brothers)
Duet	Kenny Rogers and Dottie West
Band	Oak Ridge Boys Band
Country TV Show	"Live From The Grand Ole Opry"
Gospel Act	Connie Smith
Founders' Award	Pee Wee King

1980

Male Artist	Marty Robbins
Female Artist	Loretta Lynn
Most Promising Male Artist	Hank Williams, Jr
Most Promising Female Artist	Charly McClain
Songwriter	Marty Robbins
Single	"Coward Of The County" (Kenny Rogers, artist; Roger Bowling and Billy Edd Wheeler, writers)
Bluegrass Group	Bill Monroe and the Blue Grass Boys
Musician	Roy Clark
Comedy Act	The Statler Brothers
Vocal Group	The Statler Brothers
Album	"The Originals" (The Statler Brothers)
Duet	Conway Twitty and Loretta Lynn
Band	Charlie Daniels
Country TV Show	"Live From The Grand Ole Opry"
Gospel Act	The Carter Family
Founders' Award	Buck Owen

1981

Male Artist	George Jones
Female Artist	Barbara Mandrell
Most Promising Male Artist	Boxcar Willie
Most Promising Female Artist	Louise Mandrell
Songwriter	Curly Putnam and Bobby Braddock
Single	"He Stopped Loving Her Today" (George Jones, artist; Curly Putnam and Bobby Braddock, writers)
Bluegrass Group	Bill Monroe and The Blue Grass Boys
Musician	Barbara Mandrell
Comedy Act	The Mandrell Sisters

Vocal Group	The Statler Brothers
Album	"Tenth Anniversary" (The Statler Brothers)
Duet	Conway Twitty and Loretta Lynn
Band	The Marty Robbins Band
Country TV Show	"Barbara Mandrell and The Mandrell Sisters"
Gospel Act	The Hee Haw Gospel Quartet
Founders' Award	Betty Cox Adler

1982

Male Artist	Marty Robbins
Female Artist	Barbara Mandrell
Most Promising Male Artist	T.G. Sheppard
Most Promising Female Artist	Shelly West
Duet	David Frizzell and Shelly West
Band	Alabama
Vocal Group	The Statler Brothers
Musician	Barbara Mandrell
Country TV Show	"Barbara Mandrell and The Mandrell Sisters"
Single	"Elvira" (The Oak Ridge Boys, artist; Dallas Frazier, writer)
Album	"Feels So Right" (Alabama)
Bluegrass Group	Ricky Skaggs Band
Gospel Act	The Hee Haw Gospel Quartet
Comedy Act	The Statler Brothers

1983

Male Artist	Marty Robbins
Female Artist	Janie Fricke
Star Of Tomorrow	Ricky Skaggs
Duet	David Frizzell and Shelly West
Band	Alabama
Vocal Group	Alabama
Album	"Come Back To Me" (Marty Robbins)
Single	"Some Memories Just Won't Die" (Marty Robbins, artist; B. Springfield, writer)
Bluegrass Group	Ricky Skaggs Band
Comedy Act	The Statler Brothers
Gospel Act	The Hee Haw Gospel Quartet
Country Music TV Series	"Hee Haw"
Country Music TV Special	"Conway Twitty On The Mississippi"
Living Legend	Roy Acuff

THE WORDS DON'T FIT THE PICTURE

Hit songs that sparked movies of the same name, and vice versa

Coal Miner's Daughter
: Loretta Lynn's autobiographical song developed first into a book, then, in 1980, into one of the warmest of Country music biopics with Sissy Spacek giving a superb performance in the title role.

High Noon
: Tex Ritter rendered the Ned Washington and Dmitri Tiomkin title song to this classic western, his singing providing a perfect counterpoint to the screen action.

True Grit
: A hit for Glen Campbell, who also appeared in the movie, playing sidekick to John Wayne, who won an Oscar for his performance as the unstoppable, one-eyed Rooster Cogburn.

Ode to Billy Joe
: Just when everybody thought it safe to go back on Tallahachie Bridge, Max Baer made a film based on Bobbie Gentry's 1967 hit. Shame really.

Little Fauss and Big Halsy
: Johnny Cash got not only a title song but a whole soundtrack album out of this one, a biker movie headed by a great duo – Robert Redford and Michael J. Pollard – though one which became ultimately dubbed "a sort of Batman And Robin on wheels."

Your Cheatin' Heart
: Hank Williams Jr sang the title song and others while George Hamilton portrayed Hank Sr in the most jollied-up screen biog of all time. Are you sure Hank done it this way?

Waterhole Three
: Zany but worthwhile comedy that found Roger Miller delivering his equally daffy "Ballad Of Waterhole Three" offscreen while hero James Coburn, who defines rape as "assault with a friendly weapon," spends his onscreen time searching for gold.

9 to 5
: Three secretaries gang up on their overbearing boss. A sometimes amusing tale which provided Dolly Parton not only with a leading role but also a No.1 pop hit in the form of the title song.

167

Harper Valley P.T.A.	Another song-sparked movie that appeared belatedly – ten years after the Jeannie C. Riley hit that provided its reason for living. A box-office success nevertheless.
I Walk The Line	Johnny Cash's early hit was bound to inspire someone in Hollywood to connect in some way or another. Luckily, it was John Frankenheimer who, in 1970, was moved to utilize the song in a movie about Tennessee moonshiners.
Convoy	C.W. McCall's C.B. hit of 1976 sparked off a Peckinpah-directed trucker epic of the same name just two years later.

A scene from Convoy

YOU AND ME

Country stars by other Country stars

Tom T. Hall by Bobby Bare

"Tom used to give me some of his best songs and if he hadn't started recording I'd probably have gotten 'Old Dogs, Children And Watermelon Wine,' which is a great song. We're very close friends but the problem is that whenever we get together he always wants to drink brandy – and after three shots of brandy I'm always drunk. However, he talks me into it by saying things like 'It's only fruit juice, Bobby Joe.' But that fruit juice, it wipes me out quick. Soon I find that I'm talking to myself!"

Shel Silverstein by Stella Parton

"He's a very talented man, a great person, a jewel. He's not only very artistic but also very sensitive. I guess he's an eccentric though – sometimes he comes into the office and maybe he'll have a shirt on that looks as if it came right out of the garbage can. And when he comes to the studio, when you happen to be recording some of his songs, he'll just sit there, drawing cartoons. They're so good. Perhaps one day I'll get to use one on the front of one of my albums – that way, maybe, I'll have a sleeve that'll flatter me."

George Richey by Tammy Wynette

"Richey – I call him Richey – came to Nashville about the same time as me. He became close friends with Billy Sherrill, Al Gallico, Norro Wilson and a lot of other people that I knew. He also started writing songs with Billy and recorded a lot of people I knew and eventually began producing my songs whenever Billy was out of town or working with somebody else. We became the best of friends, big buddies. And I guess I cried on his shoulder more than anybody's when George (Jones) went off drinking someplace. He was the one who always went looking for George – though he rarely ever found him! – and after Richey's marriage was through and I got my divorce, we started going out to dinner together, spending lots of time together. And then we became more than buddies."

Elvis Presley by Jerry Naylor

"Elvis was incredible. I worked with him on his first tour, the one on which he, Scotty Moore and Bill Black all came out in a '51 Lincoln that could barely make the tour. Elvis was making eighty dollars a night then and I was earning seventy-five. Even in those days, whenever he walked onstage there was no question that you were watching a giant. Even Hank Snow wouldn't follow him. Later, I worked with Elvis on another early show that had the most incredible line-up. I can't remember exactly where it was, Odessa, San Angelo . . . somewhere in West Texas, anyway. But on that show there was Johnny Horton, The Wilburn Brothers, Carl Belew, Roy Orbison, Johnny Cash, Bob Luman, my group The Cavaliers, and Elvis. If I remember rightly, that was about the time he bought his first pink Cadillac and made all the West Texas boys so jealous they filled the gas tank with sugar!"

Hank Thompson by Roy Clark

"He's the coolest man I know. That man can't be rushed. He can be fifty miles away with three minutes to curtain – and he just glides."

Kinky Friedman
by David Allan Coe

"These days, Kinky's in New York and playing the Lone Star Cafe pretty regularly. He goes to acting school and he's also getting involved in films. But he hasn't made any records lately – you gotta understand that the music business is basically run by Jewish people and the image thrown up by Kinky Friedman and The Texas Jewboys was not something that they wanted to promote."

Jerry Lee Lewis by Mickey Gilley

"Jerry Lee is Jerry Lee and everybody knows all about him. Being his cousin helps in some ways but hinders in others. It hindered because everybody thought I was copying him and I had to keep saying that my style was something that just came naturally because he and I grew up together. I've been trying to get an album together with Jerry Lee for a while now and our record companies have agreed that we can do it. I think it would be a feather in my hat if I can get him to do it – at Gilley's if possible. Now all I've got to do is to get him in a corner and tell him we've got permission. He told me he'd do it so now's the time he can either put up or shut up!"

Glen Campbell by Carl Jackson

"He's great, y'know – one of the best guitarists I've ever seen in my life and definitely one of the greatest singers. He plays a lot of jazz guitar, some of the best jazz guitar you'll ever hear. And though people know he plays guitar, they don't realize just what he can play. I'd really like to be like Glen, someone who's respected in all fields and able to have hits in both pop and Country."

170   Stella Parton   Kinky Friedman   Carl Jackson

YOU'RE LOOKING AT COUNTRY

The final list

Every list heading through *The Country Music Book of Lists* has been a song title. Below we show the Country artist's name most usually associated with each particular title.

Joe Stampley	**ALL THESE THINGS**
Skeeter Davis	**AM I THAT EASY TO FORGET?**
Marty Robbins	**AMONG MY SOUVENIRS**
Johnny Ashcroft	**AND THE BAND PLAYED WALTZING MATILDA**
Mel Tillis	**COMMERCIAL AFFECTION**
Hank Locklin	**THE COUNTRY MUSIC HALL OF FAME**
Dobie Gray	**DRIFT AWAY**
Roger Miller	**ENGLAND SWINGS**
Porter Wagoner	**EVERYTHING I'VE ALWAYS WANTED**
Bobby Bare	**FIND OUT WHAT'S HAPPENING**
Ray Price	**FOR THE GOOD TIMES**
George Hamilton IV	**FORT WORTH, DALLAS OR HOUSTON**
Roy Rogers	**A FOUR-LEGGED FRIEND**
Kris Kristofferson	**GETTING BY HIGH AND STRANGE**
Dave and Sugar	**GOLDEN TEARS**

Moe Bandy	**HANK WILLIAMS YOU WROTE MY LIFE**
Sonny James	**HOLD WHAT YOU'VE GOT**
Hank Williams	**HONKY TONK BLUES**
Hank Williams	**HONKY TONKIN'**
Lefty Frizzell	**IF YOU'VE GOT THE MONEY, I'VE GOT THE TIME**
Johnny Cash	**I GOT STRIPES**
Boxcar Willie	**I LOVE THE SOUND OF A WHISTLE**
Patsy Cline	**IMAGINE THAT**
Tommy Cash	**I'M GONNA WRITE A SONG**
Merle Haggard	**I TAKE A LOT OF PRIDE IN WHAT I AM**
Hank Snow	**I'VE BEEN EVERYWHERE**
Con Hunley	**I'VE BEEN WAITING FOR YOU ALL OF MY LIFE**
Don Williams	**I'VE GOT A WINNER IN YOU**
Maury Finney	**I WANT TO PLAY MY HORN ON THE GRAND OLE OPRY**
Barbara Mandrell	**I WAS COUNTRY WHEN COUNTRY WASN'T COOL**
Don Gibson	**A LEGEND IN MY TIME**
George Jones and Melba Montgomery	**LET'S GET TOGETHER**
James O'Gwynn	**MY NAME IS MUD**
Tom T. Hall	**OLD DOGS, CHILDREN & WATERMELON WINE**
Johnny Cash	**ONE PIECE AT A TIME**
Jim Ed Brown	**POP A TOP**
Willie Nelson	**REMEMBER ME**
Anne Murray	**SING HIGH, SING LOW**
Chris LeDoux	**SING ME A SONG, MR RODEO MAN**

Merle Haggard	**SING ME BACK HOME**
Roy Acuff	**SO MANY TIMES**
Mel Tillis	**SOMETHING SPECIAL**
Waylon Jennings	**SOMETHING'S WRONG IN CALIFORNIA**
Johnny Paycheck	**TAKE THIS JOB AND SHOVE IT**
Red Foley	**TENNESSEE SATURDAY NIGHT**
Gene Autry	**THAT'S WHY I LEFT THE MOUNTAINS**
Bob Wills	**TIME CHANGES EVERYTHING**
Gib Guilbeau	**TOE TAPPIN' MUSIC**
Don Williams	**TULSA TIME**
Ray Stevens	**TURN YOUR RADIO ON**
Ray Pillow	**VOLKSWAGEN**
Larry Gatlin and The Gatlin Brothers	**WE'RE NUMBER ONE**
Statler Brothers	**WHATEVER HAPPENED TO RANDOLPH SCOTT?**
Bill Anderson	**WHERE HAVE ALL OUR HEROES GONE?**
Kris Kristofferson	**WHY ME?**
Elvis Presley	**WILD IN THE COUNTRY**
Bobby Bare	**THE WINNER**
Willie Nelson	**THE WORDS DON'T FIT THE PICTURE**
Kitty Wells and Red Foley	**YOU AND ME**
Loretta Lynn	**YOU'RE LOOKING AT COUNTRY**

Acknowledgements   Hello and thank you to all of the Country artists who took time from their busy schedules to contribute to this book.

Thanks also to Kathy Gangwisch, Robin Wolkey, Tony Byworth, Sarah Sherrill, Linda Emerson, Cindy Leu, Debbie Banks, Martha Haggard, Jerry Bailey, Janice Azrak, Cathy Philips, Loudilla, Loretta and Kay Johnson, Mary Reeves, Judy Newby, Jennifer Bohler, Max Ellis, Manfred Vogel, Fran Boyd, Terry Lott, Joanna Burns, Sue Foster, Judy Lipsey, Roy Carr, Chris Diwell, Donna Jean Smith, Kathy McClintock, Julie Henry, Jana Talbot, Kathy Gurley, Tom Adkinson, Susan Hackney, Cynthia Spencer, Patrick Humphries, Don Wick, Lee Rector, Bob Oermann, John Lomax III and Clare Chetwood.